MW01623044

The CONDO and CO-OP *Handbook*

R. Dodge Woodson

The CONDO and CO-OP *Handbook*

A Comprehensive Guide to
Buying and Owning a Condo or Co-op

R. DODGE WOODSON

MACMILLAN • USA

Macmillan Spectrum
An imprint of MACMILLAN USA
A Simon & Schuster Macmillan Company
1633 Broadway
New York, NY 10019-6785

Copyright © 1998 by R. Dodge Woodson

Macmillan Publishing books may be purchased for business or sales promotional use. For information please write: Special Markets Department, Macmillan Publishing USA, 1633 Broadway, New York, NY 10019

All rights reserved. No part of this book shall be reproduced, stored in a retrieval system, or transmitted by any means, electronic, mechanical, photocopying, recording, or otherwise, without written permission from the publisher. No patent liability is assumed with respect to the use of the information contained herein. Although every precaution has been taken in the preparation of this book, the publisher and author assume no responsibility for errors or omissions. Neither is any liability assumed for damages resulting from the use of information contained herein. For information, address Spectrum, 1633 Broadway, 7th Floor, New York, NY 10019-6785.

MACMILLAN is a registered trademark of Prentice-Hall, Inc.

International Standard Book Number 0-02-861811-4
Library of Congress Catalog Card Number: 98-85450

01 00 99 98 4 3 2 1

Interpretation of the printing code: the rightmost number of the first series of numbers is the year of the book's printing; the rightmost number of the second series of numbers is the number of the book's printing. For example, a printing code of 98-1 shows that the first printing occurred in 1998.

Printed in the United States of America

Designer: Scott Meola

Dedication

This book is dedicated to Adam and Afton—
the special people in my life.

Contents

Contents at a Glance

CHAPTER 4: *Taxes and Legal Issues*

Many people buy a home for tax advantages. Owners of condos see their tax savings in a way similar to traditional home ownership. Co-op owners derive tax benefits in a different way. This chapter explains why and how tax savings may benefit the owners of both condos and co-ops. Legal issues for people owning condos and co-ops can be complex. Unlike owning a single-family home, having a deed to a condo or a lease on a co-op can bring special legal implications into play. Some of these considerations are discussed in this chapter.

CHAPTER 5: *Common Space, Repairs and Restrictions*

As an owner of a condo or co-op, you are required to participate in the maintenance and management of common space. This chapter explains what common space is and gives several examples of what might be considered common space, such as tennis courts, hallways, balconies, and other amenities. When repairs are needed to maintain common space, individual owners may be assessed special fees to cover the cost of repair expenses. In some cases, this can involve a large amount of money. This chapter shows you how to understand and prepare for these expenses.

Restrictions are usually placed on owners of condos and co-ops. An owner of a condo can normally redecorate interior living space to personal tastes, but this is not the case with anything seen from outside the condo, including the hall side of a door, a mailbox, or landscaping. Co-op owners may be prevented from having pets in their dwelling unit. This chapter discusses the long list of likely restrictions to make you aware of what questions to ask and what fine print to look for.

CHAPTER 6: *Condos Versus Co-ops: Pros and Cons*

This chapter contains numerous examples showing the advantages and disadvantages of owning a condo or buying into a cooperative apartment building. In addition to describing the individual pros and cons of each, it compares condos to co-ops, pointing out the strong points and the drawbacks. If you are confused or undecided about which type of unit to buy, this chapter may help you make up your mind.

CHAPTER 7: *Buying New or Used, You Need the Right People to Work With*

There are three basic ways for prospective buyers to find and negotiate the sale of a condo or co-op. Real estate brokers can be used in the same role that they play for single-family homes. This chapter discusses the advantages and disadvantages of working with brokers, and includes a complete discussion on the subject of working with buyer's brokers.

Buying directly from a developer can result in lower prices; but the risk of dealing directly with a developer can be great for a novice buyer. This chapter points out good reasons for dealing with developers and shows you how to protect yourself if you are not under the guidance of a buyer's broker. Buying a unit directly from a live-in owner is another good way to save money, but it can be risky. A full discussion on the risks and rewards of dealing directly with live-in owners finishes out this chapter.

CHAPTER 8: *Inspecting, Evaluating and Rating Potential Purchases*

Inspecting a condo or co-op before purchasing it is a critical step in achieving safe, affordable ownership. Property inspections are a good idea for all real estate purchases, but they can be particularly important when buying into a cooperative project. Since a shareholder of a co-op corporation is responsible for his or her share of all maintenance and repair costs, the condition of a building can have a lot to do with what the new owner will have to pay in excess of scheduled lease payments. Condo owners who are assessed fees for the upkeep and repair of big-ticket items, like swimming pools, recreation halls, and so forth are also at risk when a property is not in good condition. After a complete inspection of a property is made, the perspective buyer must evaluate and rate the findings. Besides discussing the information presented above, this chapter shows you how to use a simple checklist to evaluate and rate every unit you are considering for purchase. In doing this, you can protect yourself from hidden costs and financial nightmares.

CHAPTER 9: *Negotiating and Contracting the Purchase*

As popular as condos are and as prolific as co-ops are becoming, a good negotiator can often buy either type of living space well below market value. There is almost always a developer or a live-in resident dying to make a deal. This chapter informs you of the many effective negotiating strategies that work well with common-space properties, as well as gives you a complete rundown on what to expect during the purchase-and-sale paperwork. Tips are provided on what should and shouldn't be included in a contract to purchase. Contract terms and phrases, such as "Time is of the essence" are explained to protect you from the little word tricks that some sellers use to gain leverage in a sale.

CHAPTER 10: *Financing Factors*

Financing a condo or co-op can be done in a manner similar to that used with single-family homes; however, there can be differences involved in the financing of common-space properties. This chapter discusses qualifying ratios, types of loans, mortgage clauses, owner financing, and so forth. You will see why you should never buy real estate or corporate shares with an installment contract or on a bond-for-deed basis. Sellers sometimes offer owner financing when they cannot legally do so. If a seller has a "Due on sale" clause in a mortgage agreement, a new buyer taking advantage of owner financing can lose a small fortune in money and not have a place to live. This type of information, with a complete explanation and examples, will be given throughout the chapter.

CHAPTER 11: *Seeing Your Home as an Investment*

Condo and co-ops are often purchased as starter homes. This means that owners will sell their units as their incomes and family sizes grow. Elderly buyers turn to condos and co-ops to avoid physical maintenance and repair work. This type of buyer must prepare for living on less as age becomes more of a factor and income drops off. Single people frequently consider condos and co-ops as an affordable alternative to renting where tax savings can be had. In all of these cases, the owners should look at their homes as investments. This chapter highlights the investment potential of both condos and co-ops. It also provides a basis on which to rate the risk and return on such an investment. Buying a home is always an investment, but some deals do better than others, and this chapter shows you how to get the most out of their cost-of-living dollar.

CHAPTER 12: *When You Are Ready To Sell*

A majority of condo and co-op owners reach a point where they want to move up to larger living conditions. This often means selling out of their existing home, but it doesn't have to. Condos and co-ops make great rental properties. An owner may benefit from retaining ownership and renting their space out to others while living in a new home. This angle is discussed in detail. If a straight sale is wanted, a seller may have to invest a little time, effort, and money to see a strong sales price. This chapter shows you how to sell a condo or co-op quickly and profitably in any real estate market.

GLOSSARY

This contains real estate words, terms, and phrases.

Acknowledgments

I'd like to thank my agent, Jake Elwell, of Wieser & Wieser, Inc. for making this book possible for me. A special thanks goes out to my mom and dad for their support of my real estate endeavors over the years.

Chapter 1

Definitions and Differences of Condos and Co-ops

Condos and co-ops are very similar in many ways, but they differ greatly in others. Before you buy either of these types of properties, there is much you should evaluate. Neither is the best home for everyone. However, both offer advantages to specialized owners. The two types of living space are often considered the same. They are not. You must know the differences between the two before you can make a wise buying decision.

Condominiums and cooperative apartments are still relatively new to the real estate market. They have both been around for decades, but they are not as common as single-family homes. A number of home buyers don't know the inner workings of either of these types of living environment. Condos have a gained a good bit of glory since the '70s, but co-ops are still fairly unknown, except in major city markets.

Signing a contract to buy real estate is a huge step in a person's life. Once you commit to buying a home, you are in for some rewards, some risks, and certainly, some surprises. It is essential for you to have a clear understanding of what you are doing before you do it. Real estate brokers can help, but they might push you a little faster than you are prepared to go. Use this chapter as a primer of what to expect if you go shopping for a condo or co-op. The smartest home buyers are those who are well informed. This entire book is dedicated to making you a market-savvy buyer who will make fewer mistakes and enjoy richer rewards from your real estate purchase.

THE DIFFERENCE BETWEEN A CONDO AND A CO-OP

There is one basic difference between a condominium and a co-op. When you buy a condo, you get a deed of ownership. Buying a co-op doesn't give you this. Instead, you become a shareholder in a corporation that owns the entire building where your co-op apartment is housed. On the surface, this may not seem like a very significant difference. Whether you live in a condo or a co-op, you are basically buying the air space within your living unit. There are other similarities, which we will discuss shortly, but the big difference comes in the form of ownership.

BUY A CONDO, GET A DEED
BUY A CO-OP, GET SHARES OF STOCK

WHAT IS A CONDOMINIUM?

What is a condominium? A condominium is a type of residential housing. It can provide shelter for full-time living, vacation use, or rental income. Investors often buy condominiums in resort areas because of the large rental income they can produce. Condos are popular with first-time buyers, because this type of living unit is frequently much less expensive than a detached home. People who are retiring look to condos because of their price and low maintenance. As you are starting to see, there are many types of buyers for condominiums. But, what are you buying when you buy a condo?

If you buy a condominium, you are buying the air space within a portion of a building that is owned by someone else. *Air space* is the space within a dwelling where air circulates. In other words, if you are in your dwelling and breathing air, the space containing that air belongs to you. This may sound frightening, but read on. The air space you purchase is deeded to you, and the deed is recorded in the local hall of records. This amounts to true ownership of something tangible. In addition to your air space, you own an undivided interest in the surrounding real estate, such as hallways, walls, roofs, parking lots, and so forth.

Essentially, a condo is a glorified apartment-style home where you own the floor coverings, the wall coverings, and the ceiling coverings, as well as all the air space within these confines. You own the wall covering, whether it be paint or wallpaper, but you don't own the wall, at least not exclusively. This type of ownership is confusing to many people, so don't feel bad if it takes you a while to catch onto the concept. Trust me, you will understand all aspects of your purchase by the time you finish this book.

Additionally, you have an ownership interest in the common areas. The terms "common areas" or "common elements" can cover a wide variety of items and areas. These can include land, buildings, amenities (such as swimming pools and tennis courts), plumbing, wiring, roofs, windows, and other construction components. The downside of having a piece of the ownership for the common areas and elements is maintenance. The cost of this maintenance is shared by all owners within the building, and you will be responsible for your share. Keep in mind, condo ownership is a fairly complicated subject and you are getting only a basic overview at the moment. We will go into specific details along our path to your successful ownership of a condo or co-op.

In addition to your deeded air space and your undivided interest in common elements and areas, you may own a portion of limited common elements. An example of this could be a balcony or deck. Since this appurtenance is outside of your dwelling, you do not own it entirely. However, it is reserved for your personal and private use. A personal garage unit for your dwelling could be another example of this type of limited common element. Even though the appurtenance is owned by the condominium community, you have the right to exclusive use of it. While all owners in the community can use the swimming pool, playground, or tennis court, your balcony and garage are for your use only. Common elements and areas are discussed at greater length in Chapter 5, "Common Space, Repairs, And Restrictions."

Condos come in all shapes and sizes. They are often thought of as converted apartment buildings, but this is only one form of condominium development. A condo can resemble a townhouse, an apartment, or even share many characteristics with a single-family home that has close neighbors. Some professional buildings are built as condos, but this book concentrates on the residential aspects of this form of real estate.

There are many differences between condominiums and single-family homes, but there are also a good number of similarities. For example, you get a deed to real property when you buy either type of property. You will pay property taxes on your living unit with either a condo or a single-family home. Both condos and single-family homes can be mortgaged. Tax deductions that are allowable for home ownership apply to condos just as they do to single-family residences. One big difference is the exterior of the building where you live. As a condo owner, you have limited options for changes to the exterior appearance of a condo. The flip side is that you don't have to foot the full bill for repairs and upkeep on your own. There are, to be sure, pros and cons to consider.

What are you getting when you buy a condo?

- A deed to real property
- Ownership of the air space within your living unit
- Partial ownership in common areas
- Probable tax deductions
- Responsibilities for a portion of maintenance and repairs

A ROUGH SKETCH OF CONDO DETAILS

A rough sketch of condo details can reveal answers which you may find favorable or distasteful. If you think that buying a condo is the same as buying a townhouse or detached home, think again. Townhomes and detached homes can be governed by a number of rules found in deed covenants and restrictions, but this is not always true. Condos, on the other hand, are almost always governed by strict rules for exterior improvements. This, in itself, may be a turn-off to you. But, before you pass judgment, get all of the facts. Let me give you some examples of what I'm talking about.

Features of a condo

- Stability
- Security
- Tax advantages
- Pride in ownership

- Privacy
- Potential equity gain
- Investment potential

STABILITY

The stability of any real estate situation can be questionable. Historically, real estate has been a good investment. Condominiums also fall into this category. Generally speaking, condos are a stable investment. Some developments do better than others, but this is true of single-family homes, as well. Depending upon the status of the development into which you are buying, you may be able to get a good picture of the project's track record.

We will talk more later about risk and investment, but for now, let's concentrate on some key issues involving stability. If you buy your condo *"in the dirt"*—which means buying it from plans and blueprints before it is built—you are at a higher risk level than you would be if you were buying an established unit. The good side of this situation is that if the project takes off and flies, you stand to see a substantial gain in your property value and net worth.

Buying an existing, established condo reduces your financial risk and allows you to check past performance on the project. You can investigate association fees and how they have increased over the years. A maintenance schedule should be available for your review. The sales of other units is a matter of public record, so you can track down the financial success of previous owners. When you want to be safe and secure, you should shop for your new residence in established neighborhoods.

A MISSED OPPORTUNITY

Many years ago, around 1977, I came upon a deal that seemed fantastic. It was an apartment building being converted to condominiums in Annandale, Virginia. I walked through one of the model units and wanted to buy into the project. Condos were fairly new at the time, and most people were leery of them. I went to my parents for a loan, but they declined my request, saying that condos were too risky. Then I went to an investor I knew and tried to make a deal. He told me the project would be bankrupt in less than a year. Nobody believed in my intuition on this project.

As it turned out, I was unable to buy a unit in the condo conversion. Marketing for the project picked up several months later, and the place was a hit. In less than two years, the price of the units had doubled, and they were still going up. To this day, I tease my parents about doubting my instincts about the purchase. If they, or someone, had helped me, I could have made tens of thousands of dollars in less than two years while having a nice place to live. As it turned out, my condo venture was the one that got away. But, this is the type of reward that exists in some circumstances.

Security

Security is an issue that continues to be of great importance. Unfortunately, crime occurs everywhere. It happens on the sidewalks of Los Angeles and in the remote woods of northern Michigan. A person is being mugged on a subway in New York while a camper's electric generator is being stolen in Maine. The crimes are different, but the need for security exists in both environments.

Buying a home in a safe neighborhood is comforting. But, what constitutes a safe neighborhood? Are condos as safe as single-family homes? It's not unlikely that a quality condominium offers better occupant security than a single-family residence. If there is safety in numbers, you have an advantage by living in a condo. Some condos offer full-time security patrols and surveillance systems. Getting this type of protection in a detached home would be very expensive. Not all condos are security conscious, but many are.

Tax Advantages

How are the tax advantages when you own a condo? They are comparable, in scope, to what you would have with a single-family home. The ownership of a condominium is treated with the same tax principals that are applied to detached housing. Each individual has a different tax status, so check with an experienced professional before you make assumptions about tax savings. Over all, though, you should be able to enjoy the same tax benefits with a condo as you would with a single-family home. Taxes are discussed more fully in Chapter 4, "Taxes And Legal Issues."

Pride in Ownership

Some people place more emphasis on pride in ownership than do others. There are people who believe that condominiums are not prestigious. Some condos fit that description, but others are very luxurious. Like single-family homes, condos come in all conditions and in various locations. Physical condition and location both play a vital role in the outward appearance of a home. If you buy a condo under the right conditions, there is no reason why you shouldn't take pride in your ownership of the unit.

Privacy

Privacy is something that you must relinquish, at least to some extent, when you buy a condo. Your neighbors are going to be close by. However, you might have only one neighbor in an adjoining unit. Some condos are built like duplex apartments. This means you have one neighbor on the other side of your living space, and then there is some ground between you and the next unit. More often, however, condo living can be compared to life in an apartment.

There are certain aspects of condominium living to which you might need to become accustomed. You may not be allowed to wash your car in your driveway. Laying out in the sun to get a tan may attract a crowd. It's very possible that you will hear a neighbor's television or radio from time to time. You can't expect to live in an urban environment, with neighbors only a wall away, and enjoy the same privacy that you would on twenty-five acres in the country.

For the disadvantage of lost privacy, you gain an advantage. You have neighbors to call upon if you need help. If you have children (and if your condo association permits children), they will likely have playmates within the project to spend time with. It reminds me of something I learned in school: for every action, there is an equal but opposite reaction.

Potential Equity Gain

What can you expect in terms of equity gain from a condo? There is no way to know what real estate will do from one year to the next. Historically, real estate increases in value. Some developments appreciate faster than others. This is true of all types of housing. The only way you can judge your equity gain is to look at the track record of a development. It's best if you have at least ten years of performance to consider. Projects often appreciate rapidly when they are first built, but then they may slow down in their economic growth. Condos are not as prone to individual equity gains as single-family homes, but you should see some gains. It is possible, however, that your condo will soar above the rest of the local market. Too many factors come into play to draw a hard and fast line on equity gain for any single property.

Investment Potential

What is the investment potential of a condo? It can be quite good. Like all real estate investments, condos come with their share of risks for an investor. The low initial cost of a condo makes it an attractive investment consideration. Buying "in the dirt" can result in quick equity gains and huge profits for a short period of time. However, if a project doesn't gain favor with the public, an investor's money can be tied up for years before a sizable return is seen.

In the right locations, such as along a beach or atop a mountain ski slope, condos can turn into gold mines for savvy investors. To make money in real estate, you must do a lot of research. You must also have patience and be willing to hold onto your investment until it is ripe. Timing is often one of the most crucial elements of profitable real estate investing. If you are looking for an affordable real estate investment, condos are certainly worth considering.

THE ASSOCIATION

The association organization for a condo project can vary greatly in scope, direction, and administration. Yet, all condominiums are guided by some form of association. An *association,* or management structure, is formed when a property is declared a condominium. The document that is usually used to establish a condominium is often called a *declaration.* The declaration is prepared by the association's board. The association is run by a board of directors, not too unlike a corporation. Some associations refer to their board of directors as a board of

> **ARE CONDOS SAFE INVESTMENTS?**
>
> It's difficult to say whether any investment will be a safe one. Condominiums have been around long enough and are well-accepted enough that they should provide you with an average safety factor. They are not a fad that is here today and gone tomorrow. Are they as safe as a detached home? Maybe yes, and maybe no. Condominiums are more appealing to a lot of people than detached homes are. To find out more about the investment angle of condos and co-ops, read Chapter 11, "Seeing your Home as an Investment."

managers. You, as a condo owner, participate in the selection of the people who make up your association. People who serve on the board are typically condo owners within the development.

The board of directors shoulders a lot of responsibility and often takes a lot of heat from other owners. It is not always an enviable position to hold. Some of what the board members must do is budget for, arrange, and oversee maintenance duties. Requests from condo owners for improvements and changes must be reviewed by board members. Any of these duties can draw fire from unhappy owners. Let me give you some examples of this.

If you want to replace the carpeting in your condo, you can. When you decide to repaint your living room walls, you can do it without asking for anyone's permission. However, if you decide that a brass light fixture would look better by your front door than the black one that the condo came with, you had better be careful. I'm not talking only about the possibility of electrical shock. The association may prohibit you from replacing the existing light fixture with any other type of fixture. Not all associations carry this much power, but many do.

Exterior light fixtures don't belong to you entirely. They are a part of what you have a common, undivided interest in. This means that in many cases, you cannot change the light without first getting permission from the association. The same could apply if you wanted a different mail box, new house numbers, or even adding a brass kick plate to your front door. Before condo owners can do anything to the outside of their buildings, they must usually obtain permission from the board of directors.

The reason for tight exterior controls is, in effect, for your protection. It prohibits people from lowering the property value with unusual outside additions or "improvements." This type of control by the association is not limited to condo owners. Many homeowners who live in planned communities, in single-family, detached homes, face the same situation. Developers often put covenants and restrictions in property deeds to prohibit homeowners from making radical exterior changes. For example, a homeowner may be allowed a choice of only three colors for exterior siding. Roofing materials may have to be of an asphalt material, in a color of either black or brown. Developers have a free hand when establishing their covenants and restrictions. I tell you this so that you won't feel that association control is specific only to condos. You could encounter similar rules and regulations in any subdivision.

If you cherish carefree living, you can find it in a condo, but it comes at a price. You won't have to cut grass, rake leaves, or plow snow, but you will pay association fees that are used to compensate the people who perform these chores for you and the other occupants. This fee can escalate with time; this is one risk that some people are unwilling to assume. In fact, maintenance and capital repair fees are often what turns a buyer away from a condo. If your building needs a new roof, you will be expected to pay your share. We will talk more about these fees and the risks that run with them later in Chapter 2, "Condo Owner's Associations."

The Association's Power

The power of a condo association varies. In general, the influence of the condo association is substantial, and this is something you must weigh when evaluating the purchase of a condominium. Do you want other people to be in a position to control where you live and how you live? Most associations are fair, but some people just can't live under the microscope of such a situation. I'm not trying to scare you, but you should be aware of all the facts before you make a purchase.

Questions and answers about condo associations

- *Who runs condo associations?* A board of directors, also known as a board of managers.
- *Who deals with the budget for a condo association?* The board of directors.
- *When a question arises over maintenance or repairs, who decides what action should be taken?* The board of directors.
- *How much power does the association have?* An association can have considerable power, and you should know all of the bylaws and rules before you buy into an association.
- *What are association bylaws?* They are the rules you must live by, and they can be quite restrictive, so be careful.
- *Can you have pets in your new condo?* Maybe, it depends on the bylaws, rules, and regulations of your association.

- *Are children allowed in your condo?* It's possible that children are not allowed, so check it out.
- *Can you rent out your condo if you decide to move?* Maybe, but maybe not; it depends on the bylaws of your association.

It is typical for a condo association to adopt a set of bylaws. These are the laws that you, as a condo owner, must be willing to live by. Some of the laws, rules, and regulations may not meet with your approval, so inspect them carefully before you sign on the dotted line to buy a condo. To illustrate this, let me give you a few examples of the types of control to which the bylaws may apply.

When people buy homes it is not unusual for them to think that they can have pets if they want to. There are people who buy homes mostly for this reason. They are tired of landlords telling them that they can't have pets. Be advised, it is not uncommon for condo associations to address the pet issue in their bylaws. You might be limited to the size and type of pets that you can keep in your condo. It's conceivable that you will not be allowed to have pets at all. This is just one example of how strong the arm of a condo association can be. Allow me to expound upon their potential power.

It's not impossible for condo associations, in some states, to regulate the age of its inhabitants. This power varies widely, but it is possible that children of certain ages may not be allowed to reside in a condo that you buy. If you were buying a condo as a starter home in which to raise a family, this could be a real problem.

Some associations have rules pertaining to the leasing of your unit to other occupants. This may not affect you, but buying a condo as an investment and then finding that you are limited in your rental program can be a financial disaster. It is imperative that you, and preferably your legal council, review all documentation thoroughly before committing to buy a condo.

Other types of control might include a prohibition against drinking alcohol or smoking in common areas. Most occupants would consider a ruling like this favorable, but some people would be offended by it. The bottom line is this: when you buy a condo, you have to play by the rules. If you want total freedom, buy land in the country and avoid close neighbors.

CO-OPS: AN ALTERNATIVE TO CONDO LIVING

Why do people want to buy single apartments? Many people who live in large cities do. Cooperative apartments are often sold in major cities. However, the purchasers are not actually buying their perspective apartments. In reality, the buyers are purchasing shares of stock in a corporation that owns the apartments. Co-ops are not for everyone, but they fill the bill for many people.

Co-op Facts

- When you buy a co-op, you don't have a deed to real property.
- Co-op owners never actually own real estate; they own shares of stock in a corporation.
- Buying a co-op entitles you to a proprietary lease that grants you a right to reside in the co-op and to use common areas.
- As a co-op owner, you are responsible for a share of all corporate expenses that are related to the co-op development.

- Co-ops are common in big cities and rare in rural America.
- It is not unusual for co-op owners to enjoy some tax advantages from ownership.
- Co-ops are run by a board of directors.

If you buy a co-op, you will not get a deed recorded for real property. In fact, you never actually own any real property, at least not directly. The apartment you reside in is owned by a corporation. As a buyer, you own shares of stock in the corporation, but you don't own even the air space in your apartment. Yes, you can breathe the air (at least in most cities), but you can't mortgage it! This is one of the big differences between co-ops and condos.

When you buy into a co-op, you are issued a proprietary lease. This lease details your ability to reside in a certain dwelling unit and to use common areas in and around the building. As a proprietary lease holder and shareholder of the co-op corporation, you are responsible for a share of all expenses associated with the building in which you live and the grounds that surround it. If the swimming pool needs to be repainted, you have to pay a portion of the cost. If gutters need to be replaced, you must pay your part of the expense. Once you buy into a co-op, you can't call the landlord and ask him to fix things for free. As a shareholder, you own a piece of the responsibility for all expenses related to your investment property.

People often have trouble getting a clear picture of co-op ownership. One of the ways that I explain it to potential owners involves the use of role playing. Assume that you are a real estate investor. You want to buy a multi-family property for investment, but you can't afford to buy the entire property yourself. To acquire the property, you need partners—so you set up a corporation. Each partner owns a piece of the corporation that is used to buy and manage your investment property. This is the way a co-op works, except that you live in your specific unit. The corporation has the deed to the real property, and you have an interest in the corporation.

Can I Get a Loan to Buy Stock?

Can I get a loan to buy stock in a corporation? Most lenders are willing to grant loans for the purchase of co-ops. The loan you get cannot be secured by real property, as most home loans are, but many lenders will give you similar terms and conditions on a loan to buy a co-op. In most cases, the loan is secured by stock in the co-op corporation. Qualifying ration, interest rates, terms, and other elements of the loan mirror those of conventional mortgage loans, in most cases. If you have acceptable credit and the co-op you are buying into seems solid, obtaining financing should not be any more of a problem than it would be for some other type of home.

I Can't Seem to Find Any Co-ops

"I can't seem to find any co-ops, can you help me?" This is a question many real estate brokers hear. People read about co-ops and then go out looking for them. Not all areas support co-op developments. Most cooperative apartments are found in large cities. They are derived from older apartment buildings that have been converted for co-op use. Smaller cities, rural towns, and other parts of the country have not yet created co-op communities. You may not be able to find a co-op where you want to live. Condos are much more prevalent than co-ops, and even condos can be difficult to find in some regions.

Co-op Tax Savings

Will I get any tax savings if I buy into a co-op deal? Check with a tax professional, but you should be entitled to some tax breaks for the portion of certain expenses that you are required to pay as a shareholder in the corporation. There are, however, circumstances that could put your tax advantages in jeopardy. How the building is used and where the income for the corporation comes from is part of what could put you at risk. Talk with your CPA and attorney before you start spending your anticipated tax savings. In general, you should get some tax breaks as an owner of a co-op.

A Co-op's Board of Directors

The decisions for what is done with a co-op building are made by a board of directors. This is common practice for a corporation. As an owner of a co-op apartment, you will be issued stock in the corporation. The amount of stock you receive will affect your voting rights. Your stock amount affects not only your voting power, but the percentage of expenses that you must pay for building operation, maintenance, and repairs. The board of directors is made up of resident owners.

What does the Board of Directors of a Co-op Do?

- May decide to hire a management company.
- May collect rent.
- May arrange and oversee property management.
- Establishes bylaws, rules, and regulations.
- May handle evictions.
- Runs the operation of the cooperative development.

The board of directors may decide to hire a management company to run the cooperative building. This is not unusual. The management company collects rent and oversees maintenance, among other duties. You, as an owner, will pay your fair share of the management expense. Bylaws and rules apply to co-op inhabitants. Just as was discussed earlier, with condos, you may not be able to keep a pet in "your" apartment. If a freak storm occurs and all of the windows in the building are blown out, you will be assessed for your portion of the expense in replacing them. Buying a co-op is, as is the case with any home ownership, a big step and a substantial responsibility.

Eviction

Eviction is a word that you may associate with rental tenants, but not with homeowners. Don't fool yourself, you can be evicted from your own home under certain conditions. Obviously, you must be in default of some contract condition for this to happen. Eviction in detached homes is rare. Unless you ignore your house payment for months, foreclosure on your loan and the ultimate seizure of your property is not likely. But, in a co-op, you could be in for a different set of circumstances, and this is something that you should have your attorney review carefully. Let me explain.

Some co-op corporations are set up in such a way that you, as a resident/shareholder, can be evicted from your apartment for not paying your regular maintenance assessment. If this happens, your unit may be rented out until a new buyer can be found. What about your investment? It could be lost, or at least part of it might be. Co-ops do this to maintain a stable base for residents who are paying their fair share. It's a tough policy, but it seems to work. When you buy into a co-op, you have to think of yourself as a brick in a wall. You are only one component, and you need all of your neighbors to maintain your status as a

DANGER ALERT!

If you buy a co-op, you could find yourself evicted and your unit sold out from under you, without realizing any profit from the sale. This may sound crazy, but it has happened. Owners of co-ops own stock, not real property, and if you violate the bylaws of the co-op association, fail to pay your association dues, or fall into some other type of trouble, you might be put on the street with your co-op stock sold to another buyer. This is serious stuff, so be aware of your risks.

wall. If a few bricks start to fall out, the wall will soon tumble down. The strict eviction policy helps to ensure that default and destruction will not occur, therefore, protecting your investment (assuming that you are living up to your responsibilities).

Some co-op corporations are picky about who you can transfer your stock to. In other words, they may not allow you to sell your apartment to just anybody. General discrimination cannot play a factor in a co-op corporation's ruling on who can and cannot own stock, but the company can make it difficult for you to sell to a ready, willing, and able buyer. Not all co-ops do this, but it is something that you should check into before you buy a co-op.

A GENERAL CO-OP RATING SCALE

Is there a general rating scale by which you can rate co-op units? I don't think so. Co-ops exist primarily in cities like New York, Chicago, San Francisco, and Washington D.C. Many of the building are old apartment buildings. Some have been renovated to modern standards, others haven't. Each co-op building and prospectus must be considered on an individual basis. There are, however, some broad brush considerations that are typical with co-ops.

Cooperative apartments are not unlike other apartments, in terms of living conditions. You are likely to have neighbors above you, below you, and on both sides of you. Some people like this. They enjoy having friends close by. Other people detest the lack of privacy. This is a personal issue that you must address.

Space can be a problem when buying a co-op. When I say space, I mean both space in the apartment and space in the parking lot. Many people never think to ask if they will be given reserved parking in a parking lot or how many spaces they will be assigned. Many apartment buildings have been built with inadequate parking facilities. People in big cities, who use subways and taxis don't worry much about this. But, if you have your own transportation, you should ask questions pertaining to where your car can be kept and how secure it will be.

Other considerations, such as investment potential, equity gain, tax savings, and security often run about average and sometimes above average. It all depends on the building, the residents, and the co-op corporation. Each situation must be rated individually.

Condos and co-ops offer potential buyers a variety of opportunities. The two types of homes are similar, yet very different. Condominiums are better known than co-ops and are often considered a safer investment. Your personal circumstances and the region in which you live may prove that a co-op is a better alternative. Until you have all the facts, you cannot make an informed decision. Condo associations are something that many condo buyers don't understand fully. The next chapter will explain what condo associations are and how they affect the owners of condos.

Chapter 2

Condo Owner's Associations

When you buy a condominium, you will have to abide by certain rules and regulations. These stipulations are created by a developer, a board of directors, a condo association, or by all three. The implications of these rules can be severe, so don't take them lightly. This type of situation is not unique to condos. Many planned subdivisions, which contain detached, single-family homes, have associations that control certain attributes of the community. If you buy a condo, you will have to accept the rules and bylaws as they are set forth. Additionally, your living expenses may escalate each year. The added cost can come in the form of association fees.

Many prospective home buyers are unaware of the full range of costs associated with condominium living. As a real estate broker, I've worked with a number of buyers who wanted to live in condominiums. The units I've shown for sale have ranged from city units to resort units. The geographical differences may be great, but the basic principles remain the same. However, you should never make assumptions when dealing with any type of real estate. There are simply too many possibilities for differences to set a standard.

Let's say you look at one condominium development and review all of its rules and regulations. Would this give you the information you need to make a buying decision? It could be enough to influence your decision about the development you investigated, but don't use your findings as a benchmark for other developments. While there are certain laws and standards that apply to all condos, there can be dramatic differences between one project to another. You must read the fine print for each and every unit that you are considering for purchase.

> Condo living is on the rise. A 1975 report by the Department of Housing and Urban Development showed that there were approximately 14,000 condominium developments in the United States. Half of the developments were in Florida, California, and New York. A revised edition of the report, released in 1985—only ten years later—showed the number of developments to be in excess of 60,000. It was reported that some 3 million condos existed in the 60,000 projects. To go from 14,000 to 60,000 in just ten years is quite a jump.

PROFESSIONAL PURCHASING HELP

When you are seeking a condo to purchase, you should have professional help working with you. Associations, boards of directors, covenants, restrictions, and other real estate elements of your purchase are likely to be confusing. For this reason, consider hiring experts who can advise you in your best interest. Certified public accountants are experts in tax matters. Real estate attorneys are the rulers of fine print. I stress, however, that you retain a lawyer who specializes in real estate. A fantastic criminal lawyer may be a flop at deeds and contracts. Find a lawyer who has an established track record as a superior real estate wizard.

Real estate agents and brokers are beneficial in many ways. They can locate properties that you may not know are for sale. Good agents and brokers can provide you with reams of information that is helpful in making a wise decision. You should know, however, that traditional agents and brokers work for the seller of a property and with buyers. Their loyalty and fiduciary responsibility lies with the seller. Try to hire a buyer's broker to represent your interest. Buyer's brokers are sometimes paid on commission by the seller or the buyer, or by the hour. The key thing is this: a buyer's broker works for you!

Line up your professional help before you venture too far into your search for a condo. By having your players in place early, understanding contract requirements and association bylaws will be much easier. With this caveat out of the way, let's move onto the inner workings of bylaws, associations, and boards of directors.

CONDO MANAGEMENT: BY THE PEOPLE, FOR THE PEOPLE

The management of a condo project is selected by the people, for the people. Owners of condominiums within the community are selected to act as a governing body. The condominium association is supervised by this group of homeowners. Meetings are held periodically for board members to make rulings on requests from other property owners. In a sense, the board serving the condo community is similar to a zoning board that serves a small community. The condo association, which is managed by the board of directors, is the hub of the condo community.

As a condo owner, you may have some say in what and how things are done, but the association has the final say. Your ownership is limited to the air space within your unit. Personally, you have little, or no, control over exterior conditions. Technically, you don't even own the walls that separate your living space from your neighbor's. This can make you feel vulnerable, and you should feel vulnerable! Go into a condo purchase with your eyes wide open. There can be hooks hidden in the bait that will make you regret having ever considered condo life. But, don't dismiss what could turn out to be a wonderful lifestyle. Get the facts, and then make your decision.

What Your Condo Association Does

Your condo association takes care of any maintenance requirements for you. A fee is charged to you for this service, but you do not have to worry about day-to-day obligations for trash removal, snow removal, exterior painting, and so forth. If the wind blows shingles off the roof of your building, you don't have to deal with the insurance company and the roofing contractor. If a board on your balcony begins to rot, the association will have it repaired for you. All of this is done for you. This is what makes condo living so appealing to so many people. Any required maintenance outside of your air space is the responsibility of the condo association. As long as you can pay the price, you don't have to get your hands dirty. Your grass is cut for you. Someone paints lines in your parking lot for you. All you have to do is enjoy life and pay your percentage of the maintenance expense.

YOU DON'T HAVE THE HEADACHES

Condo owners don't have to cut their own grass or shovel their own snow. If you are looking for carefree living, a condo is hard to beat. You will, however, be paying for your lifestyle with regular dues and fees for the association.

The Association's Protective Role

A condo association exists, in part, for your protection. By controlling the community with certain standards, a condo association ensures that the value of the development will not deteriorate due to negligence or improper acts. This, in effect, helps to protect your real estate investment. You don't have to be concerned that your neighbor will paint a garage door pink with a black border. The association rules will not allow your neighbors to downgrade the quality of the development. It is in the association's best interest to maintain a quality community. At the same time, quality control over the development helps all residents to rest comfortably, knowing that their investments will not be harmed by the actions of their neighbors.

When you buy a house that is not under the control of an association, you have more freedom to do what you want with your property. The flip side to this is that your neighbors also have the same freedom. It doesn't take a lot for a neighborhood to deteriorate in value. If this happens, you are losing equity value in your home. To illustrate this point, let me give you a few examples of what could happen if you don't live under the guidance of an association.

I know a couple who bought a house in a nice part of town. The home is old, but the couple has fixed it up very nicely. Everything about the house and lawn looks nice. Many of the other houses along the same street are also in good repair and well kept. But, there is one house, visible from the nice house the couple lives in, where the owner has gotten creative, to say the least, with exterior paint. The house to which I'm referring has a large front porch that is supported by columns. In most cases, these columns would be painted white to complement the rest of the house. Not so for this house. The columns are painted in different colors. A pink column sits next to a blue one. Then there is a white one and a yellow one. This type of pattern continues all the way around the porch. It is not a pretty sight.

The house with the front porch can have a detrimental affect on other houses that are nearby. Radical colors on the porch columns could lower real estate appraisals for other homes. There is not much the neighbors can do about the eyesore. However, if a homeowner's association was involved, such a problem would not be allowed to exist.

Painted porch columns are not the only way for neighbors to lower the value of your home. If your neighbors don't care for their lawns, your groomed grass can make the other lawns look even worse. Again, this is something that will not happen in a condo complex. The lawn is taken care of by the association, so you don't have to be concerned about how dedicated your neighbors are when it comes to lawns and landscaping.

I'm sure that you've seen lawn ornaments from time to time. Some of them are cute. Many of the ornaments make a statement about the property owner. Too much decoration, however, can be detrimental to surrounding property values. I've seen lawns where you could hardly see any grass through all of the wooden lawn ornaments. Two particular homes come to mind as I think of this. Can you imagine living next to a neighbor who has a lawn that looks like a showroom for lawn ornaments? Well, if you buy into a condo association, you won't have to worry about this type of problem.

DANGER ALERT

Your condo association should act in the best interest of the condo community. This may clash with your personal preferences or desires. For example, the association may stipulate that dogs that weigh under 35 pounds are allowed on the property, but bigger dogs are not be tolerated. If you happen to own or want a larger dog, you're out of luck. There are many other such stipulations that can affect your lifestyle.

Evaluating Requests

One big role of the association is to evaluate requests from property owners. These requests can run the gamut—from parking an RV in the main parking lot to installing a new roof of a different type or color. Any changes you make to the exterior of your condo are likely to require board approval. This can even apply to such minor items as landscaping and light fixtures. When you buy a condo, you must be willing to accept the fact that you cannot act without approval except within the confines of your unit.

YOUR VOTE

Your vote in association decisions is based on the number of votes your unit was assigned in the declaration of the condo development. It's not unusual for condo votes to be equal among property owners, but this is not always the case. For example, a person buying a one-bedroom condo may have fewer votes in a decision than an owner of a three-bedroom condo. Find out what your voting ratio will be before you agree to buy a unit. Regardless of what your vote is, you are not a majority in and of yourself. Therefore, you have to live with the wishes of others, not unlike a presidential election. The fact that you have a vote doesn't guarantee that your wishes will be upheld. For some people, this lack of control is all it takes to rule out condo living.

SPECIAL ASSESSMENTS

The condo association to which you belong normally assesses a monthly operational fee or maintenance fee for you. This is common, but check to see how often the fee can be increased. If there is no cap (limit) to what the assessment can be each year, you could be putting yourself into a situation that will result in the loss of your home. Assuming that you are buying a condo in an established neighborhood, you can research past records to establish how much the monthly fee has gone up over past years.

DANGER ALERT!

Be aware of the risk of special assessments when you buy a condo. Some condo associations offer "caps" on their special assessments, but others don't. You could find yourself in serious financial difficulty if you are not completely aware of your responsibilities.

Monthly fees are a concern to many residents. Runaway assessments can drive a property owner into default and the loss of their property. Protect yourself against this by knowing what your worst-case scenario will be. Plan for the expense and budget your money to accommodate it. In addition to the known expense, you must be prepared for the unexpected. By the unexpected, I mean special assessments that come as a result of major deterioration or destruction. This type of problem can cut your legs right out from under you, financially speaking.

When you shop for a condo, you should inspect all aspects of the community. Look to see what condition common areas and elements are in. Is the parking lot in good shape? How does the tennis court look? Does the development maintain a community building? The reason that these considerations are important is that you may be required to kick in some cash for repairs to the common areas and elements.

A FEW THINGS TO LOOK FOR BEFORE YOU BUY A CONDO

- Check out the parking lot.
- Investigate the condition of swimming pools, tennis courts, and other amenities.
- What's the neighborhood like?

- Are the hallways well lighted?
- Will the roof of the building need to be replaced anytime soon?
- Is the siding on the building in good repair?
- Are most of the units in the development occupied?
- Review the financial statement of the association.
- What is the track record of special assessments?

Paying to have a parking area re-paved is never cheap. Replacing a tennis court can get expensive very quickly. New playground equipment can costs thousands of dollars. If a community building needs a new roof or new siding, the expense will be substantial. As a homeowner within the community, you can face a special assessment when money is needed for this type of repair or replacement. Since the cost can be quite high, you have to weigh this risk when making your decision to buy into a community that is run by an association.

DUTIES OF THE BOARD

Duties of the board of directors can involve many tasks. In some ways, you can think of the board of directors as the condo police. The board enforces rules set forth by the association. This can make life in a condo difficult for some people. Since the board is made up of residents, neighbors wind up policing each other. In doing this, some hard feelings can grow between the involved parties. When this happens, life in the community can become less enjoyable.

Each association develops its own rules, so you might not find two condo development with the same guidelines. Once the rules are put into place, it is up to the board to make sure that residents abide by them. Let's look at some examples that illustrate what a typical condo board of directors might have to deal with.

The Duties of a Condo Board of Directors

- Setting a budget
- Collecting fees
- Communicating with residents
- Paying bills for the development
- Making rules for the development
- Handling requests for property alterations
- Maintaining insurance coverage
- Overseeing maintenance requirements
- Dealing with legal obligations for the development

Setting a Budget

Setting up an operating budget and a reserve account is one of the duties of a board of directors. The board might take on this responsibility personally, or the board might hire an outside consultant to establish a viable budget. Creating a budget is not a job that is done once and forgotten. It is an ongoing responsibility.

Collecting Fees

A condo board is usually required to collect fees from residents for maintenance, management, and special assessments. This can involve as little as opening the morning mail or as much as taking legal action against residents who are in default. The board of directors is the heart of the association, and the association is the nucleus of the condo community.

Every association needs money to operate its community. If the board of directors is unable to perform properly, the entire community suffers. For example, if the board does not budget enough money for snow removal, residents will likely be charged a special assessment to keep their roads and parking areas clear of snow. When a board is ineffective in collecting regular association fees, the cash-flow of the association dwindles. This can cause decay within the community. Money is certainly one of the primary duties of a board of directors.

Communicating with Residents

The board of directors is in charge of communication with residents. It's common for an association to publish and distribute a periodical newsletter. This is one way of keeping association members informed of what's going on. When something special happens, a board of directors may call for a special meeting to communicate with residents.

Paying the Bills

Paying the bills of an association is another responsibility of the board of directors. Not only does the board have to pay the bills, records of all expenses must be kept. The records are used for tax purposes, to document expenses to residents, and to create new budgets. Running a condo association involves a lot of effort and responsibility. The board of directors for an association is, in a way, running a business.

Making Rules

Making rules for residents to obey is a duty of the board of directors. People in the community may be asked for their feelings with regards to new rules. The rules could be put up for a vote. Ultimately, however, it is the board of directors who finalizes a draft of bylaws and rules. The board is also responsible for enforcing the rules that are made.

Handling Alteration Requests

A board of directors must listen to and rule on requests for alterations. If you want to change the color of your shutters, you will most likely need approval from the board. Almost any change that is visible to the public must be approved by the board of directors. Even very simple changes can require approval. For example, let's say that you want to hang a wooden plaque next to your front door. The plaque has your last name and house number on it. As innocent as this sounds, it could require board approval.

Maintaining Insurance Coverage

It is up to the board of directors to maintain insurance coverage on the property for which the association is responsible. This includes both liability and casualty insurance. The board should shop for competitive premium rates and confirm that the coverage being carried is adequate. You, as a homeowner, should be apprised as to the type and amount of insurance coverage that is in place.

Overseeing Maintenance

The board of directors is responsible for overseeing maintenance and repair work. Is the work being performed in compliance with association rules? Are the workers insured? What is a fair price to pay for the services being rendered? For how long is the work guaranteed? These, and many other questions, should be considered by members of the board of directors.

> A report issued by the Chicago Title Insurance Company, in 1992, indicated that 13 percent of all households were condominiums. With land values increasing and raw land disappearing, the appeal of condos is likely to continue growing steadily. As people work longer hours, they are more likely to choose a maintenance-free lifestyle as a property owner.

Dealing with Legal Obligations

Legal obligations on all levels must be observed by the board of directors. It is the board who must make sure that the association is not in violation of any codes or laws. For example, if the association maintains smoke detectors in common hallways, the board must make sure that the devices are in good working order. When a lien is placed on an owner's condo as security for unpaid dues or fees, the board is in charge of the action. It is also up to the board to remove the lien once all debts have been paid.

As you can see, the board of directors for a condo development must juggle many responsibilities. The people put into power on a board must do more than simply show up for an occasional meeting. The work done by the board is critical to the success of an association. Selection of board members should be taken very seriously. Now that you have a good view of what an association is and how the board of directors works, let's talk about how this subject might affect you.

Should You Serve on the Board of Directors?

Should you serve on the board of directors for your association? The answer to this question depends upon many factors. Do you enjoy being in the spotlight? Are you good with people? Can you take criticism well? Ask yourself questions like the ones you've just read. Not everyone is meant to be a leader or decision-maker. Serving on a board of directors can make your life miserable. It can also be a rewarding experience. Only you can decide if a role in the association appeals to you.

If you are interested in being on your board of directors, assess your strengths and weaknesses. Don't take on a position for which you are not qualified. Becoming a member of the board of directors carries a lot of responsibility. If you don't take the position seriously, you can damage the quality of your development and the reputation of your board and association. You should also be willing to accept the fact that you are likely to make some enemies along the way as you perform your board functions.

HOW MANY VOTES DO CONDO OWNERS GET?

How many votes do you get as a condo owner? The answer to this question is not always as simple as you might think. Associations are set up in different ways. You can't count on every one of them to operate with identical procedures. Even if you are moving out of one condo and into a new one, you should be prepared for differences in the governmental structure of your association.

Some associations award condo owners votes based on the square footage of air space owned by the purchasers. In other words, if you have a unit with 800 square feet and your neighbor has a unit with 1,600 square feet, you might have half as much voting power as your neighbor. Some associations base voting rights on other aspects of condo ownership. For example, condos on one level may have more votes than condos on a different level. A condo that fronts on a golf course could be worth more votes than one that faces on a parking lot.

As a condo owner, you will never have enough voting power to make a difference on your own. However, the more votes

> **WHAT DETERMINES YOUR VOTING RIGHTS IN A CONDO ASSOCIATION?**
>
> Some associations award voting rights based on square footage of ownership. Your voting rights might be determined by the value of your residential unit. Check to see what your voting rights will be before you buy into an association.

you have, the louder your voting voice will be. Before you buy a condo, check to see how votes are issued. This may not seem important to you, but much of what goes on within an association is decided by votes.

WHAT TO LOOK FOR IN AN ASSOCIATION

When you are shopping for a condominium, it's helpful to know what to look for in an association. In the case of a new development, you won't have a historic track record to review. When such a record is available, you should investigate it. You can learn a lot from what has gone on in the past. For example, how often have condo fees risen, and in what amount have they risen over the years? How often has the association been over budget at the end of a fiscal year? Does the association have reserve capital compiled from a collection of annual budgets? In what condition is the accounts receivables from residents who owe money for condo fees? These are just some of the questions that you should ask before buying a condo.

Questions to Ask About Condo Associations

- Ask for and review the annual reports of the association for the last few years.

- How often have association fees gone up?
- Has the association run over budget in recent years?
- What is the amount of reserve capital in the association account?
- Are there many outstanding accounts receivable?
- In what condition are the buildings and grounds?
- Can you attend a member meeting before you buy into the association?
- Does the association own its own tools and transportation for maintenance?
- In what condition is the maintenance equipment?
- Can you review bylaws and regulations before committing to a purchase?

Review Annual Reports

When you are considering the purchase of a condo in an established community, ask the association to provide you with annual reports for the last few years. These reports will help you evaluate the management and stability of the development. You may find it desirable to have a CPA go over the reports with you. Some annual reports can be difficult to decipher.

Frequent Fee Hikes

If a condo association's fees escalate rapidly and in substantial amounts, something may be wrong with the development. The fees should go up, probably annually, but the rises should be in keeping with the rate of inflation.

Budget Woes or Reserve Capital?

An association that is routinely running out of money before the end of a fiscal year is another trouble sign. If you don't want to be charged with unexpected, special assessments, it's necessary to find an association that has control of its budget. Ideally, the association will have money reserved for unforeseen expenses. If it doesn't, major special assessments can wipe out your bank account in a hurry.

Accounts Receivable

When condo owners are paying their condo fees regularly, you are probably safe in assuming that the association works well for its property owners. On the other hand, evidence of residents who are unwilling to pay their fees indicates an association that does not serve its members well. There will almost always be some residents who are in arrears on their condo fees. This is normal. However, if you see a trend in which a lot of residents are not paying their fees as a form of protest, be careful in making a purchase.

Building and Ground Maintenance

A strong association will keep its building and grounds in good shape. This is something that you can determine easily. Walk around the buildings. Go through them if they have common hallways. Inspect the lawns and landscaping. If the buildings and grounds are well kept, you have found what should be a good association.

Attending an Association Meeting

Find out when the association is planning its next member meeting and attend the gathering. You can learn a lot by sitting in on a meeting and listening to the comments of condo owners. Some associations may prefer that their meetings be attended by owners only, but if you use your request to see a meeting as a pivotal point in your buying decision, you will probably have a seat reserved for you.

Maintenance Equipment

Many associations own their own tools and equipment. Take a look at such items as trucks, lawn mowers, and other maintenance equipment. If it looks like it is in disrepair or aging, you can expect to see some special assessments in the near future for replacing the old equipment. Not all associations maintain their own transportation, tools, and equipment. Some associations contract out all of their needs to independent contractors. The fact that an association doesn't have it's own equipment should not scare you. Independent contractors often work out to be a less expensive option in the long run.

Request a Copy of the Bylaws

Always request a copy of an association's bylaws and rules before you make a commitment to purchase a condo. Read all of the restrictions and rules carefully. Ideally, you should have your lawyer review the materials. There are so many possibilities for problems in bylaws that it is not practical to discuss all of them. Since each association has its own rules and regulations, it's impossible to have a cookie-cutter answer for what's right and wrong or good and bad. Also, what strikes you as offensive might be perfectly acceptable to someone else.

In addition to reading the association's bylaws, ask your attorney to check into the declaration of the development. This is a document that allows a development to be sold as condominium space. Some people refer to the declaration as a master deed. This document will contain covenants and restrictions that apply to the project. Of all the documentation you sift through, the declaration might be the most important.

IT'S LIKE GETTING MARRIED

Buying a condo is a little like getting married. Once you make a commitment, you are joined into a partnership that can be difficult and costly to dissolve. Shopping for a condo association and development that is right for you can take a lot of time. When you buy a condo, you are married to the association, whether you like it or not. And, the association may not be your only concern. What will your neighbors be like? Have you talked with any of them? Maybe you should. Ask residents if they are happy with their homes and their association. I realize that people in cities won't always talk to strangers, but you can probably manage to strike up a conversation with some of the residents.

Don't jump into a condo purchase. Research everything! The time you spend in evaluating a purchase is valuable, but so is the result of your work. It's easy to have a salesperson give you a grand tour and a slick presentation. Don't act on impulse or out of confusion. Get all the facts and understand them before you sign a contract to purchase a home. Buying a home is often easier than selling it, so make sure you are buying what you want.

Condominiums are solid investments in most developments. Developers, however, are sometimes fast to take advantage of a situation. Hard-case sales people may pressure you into making a buying decision right away. Incentives may be offered to you if you act fast. Don't let yourself be manipulated. Take your time. Investigate your options and consult with professionals on what type of home purchase suits your needs and desires best. You, and only you, should decide when the time is right to sign on the dotted line. Don't let some fast-talking sales pro push you into something for which you are not ready. Remember, when you buy real estate, it is for better or for worse, just like in marriage.

Chapter 3

The Corporate Workings of Co-ops

The corporate workings of a co-op is not something many people think about on a daily basis. However, if you are thinking about purchasing a cooperative apartment, you had better learn a little about the corporate structure that will be involved with your ownership. A co op is not a condo, even though a lot of people make remarks such as, "Condos, co-ops—they're all the same." There are major differences between condos and co-ops. While both types of ownership share some qualities, there are substantial differences that you should make yourself aware of.

When you buy a condo, you own something tangible. You are given a deed for the air space within your living unit. This is not the case with a co-op. In fact, co-op owners do not own real property, at all. They own shares of stock in a corporation that owns the cooperative building. If you think you will own an apartment when you buy a co-op, you're mistaken. All you own is shares in a corporation. Does this surprise you? It certainly surprises a lot of people, even people who have purchased a co-op.

Condos have become accepted as stable, and growing, forms of home ownership. Co-ops don't generally enjoy such a good reputation. Real estate experts are often quick to say that co-ops are the worst housing investment you can make. This, of course, is not always true—but there is enough evidence to lend strength to the statement.

Buying a cooperative apartment can result in a large return on your investment. This is especially true if you are a current tenant when an apartment building is being converted to cooperative use. It is common for developers to offer residing tenants substantial discounts if they buy the use of their cooperative apartment. Notice my choice of words—"buy the use of." Remember, when you buy a co-op, you are not buying the apartment. You are buying stock in the corporation that owns the apartment. I know this is repetitive information, but it is something that so many people don't understand, and I want you to have a clear idea of exactly what you are buying.

Is a co-op a good deal? It depends on many factors. As we move through this chapter, we will examine all aspects of life as a co-op owner. You will have to draw your own conclusions as to the worth of a co-op. In terms of general real estate, co-ops are typically considered to be the lowest form of home ownership. However, don't let this turn you away from what could be a good investment and a nice place to live. Review all the data before you make a decision.

HOW CO-OPS ARE CREATED

Because condos are compared with co-ops in Chapter 6, "Condos Versus Co-ops: Pros and Cons," this chapter's primary focus is to describe the procedures under which a co-op project works. It is, however, necessary for you to have a cursory understanding of where co-ops are likely to be found and how they are likely to come into existence if you are to fully understand how and why they work. For now, it is enough for you to know that co-ops are generally the result of remodeling, rather than new construction.

Where Co-ops Are Found

Most cooperative apartments are found in big cities. In this environment, co-ops are sometimes considered luxurious living. Co-op living is not held in such high standing in other parts of the country. One source indicates that only 96,000 co-ops were purchased in 1994. When you compare this statistic to the 3 million condos that were purchased in 1992, you can see that there is more demand, or availability, for condos.

People who live in metropolitan areas are accustomed to apartment life. This, I assume, is why co-ops are popular with urban dwellers. Price may be another factor. Cooperative apartments are frequently the least expensive way to get into home ownership, even though you don't technically own the home. When you combine price, lifestyle, and availability, it's easy to see why co-ops are located in heavily populated areas.

Converted Dwellings

Most cooperative apartments are made, not built. By this, I mean that co-ops are usually the result of conversions to existing apartment buildings. I'm sure some co-op projects are built from the ground up, but the majority involve the conversion of existing buildings. In some cases, very few improvements are made to the existing building at the time of conversion. Other buildings are given substantial improvements during the conversion.

Condos are frequently created with conversion projects, much in the same way that many co-ops are. But, many condo projects are built from the ground up. The demand for and money-making potential of condos is sufficient to warrant such an investment. When you buy a co-op, it is likely that you will be buying a share in an older property. It may, or may not, be modernized during the conversion process. The same could be true of a condo, but it is easier to find a new condo than it is to find a new co-op.

THE ROLE OF THE DEVELOPER

A developer is usually the person responsible for the creation of a cooperative apartment building. Co-ops are almost always apartments. Condos might be town houses, apartments, or even duplex-type designs, but co-ops are generally apartments contained under one roof. Some landlords decide to turn their rental buildings into co-ops. It is more common, however, for a developer to cut a deal with a landlord and orchestrate the conversion process. Landlords sometimes make a straight sale to a developer, and sometimes the landlord participates in the speculation of the conversion process. More often than not, you will be dealing, either directly or indirectly, with a developer when you buy into a co-op project. Chapter 7, "Buying New or Used, You Need the Right People to Work With," will provide you with more information on this subject.

The development of a co-op can progress in many ways. Sometimes a large corporation will be the developer. Other times a single individual will be the developer. It is common for a few investors to get together and form a development company, that then creates the co-op corporation. There are no hard and fast rules in the game, therefore developments can differ widely in how they are established. Here's a common scenario:

Assume that you are tired of paying rent and getting nothing but temporary shelter in return. You want to own some real estate, something to call your own. Now, let's further assume that co-ops are not popular in the area in which you wish to live. You like the co-op concept, but there are none available for sale. Do you have to settle for a condo? Not necessarily.

Let's say that you find a nice, 15-unit apartment building in a good part of town. The building is for sale, but you don't have the cash or credit to swing the purchase on your own. You do, however, have many skills that would be beneficial in the management and maintenance of the building. You have some cash and some credit, but not enough to do the deal on your own. How can you swing it? Bring in some investors.

For the sake of our example, let's say that the building is worth $750,000. Divided by the 15 units, this amounts to $50,000 a unit. Not a bad price to pay for a place to live. But, you can't buy just one unit, you have to buy the entire building. Additionally, you have to accept responsibility for all costs pertaining to the operation and maintenance of the building.

Let's further assume that a lender will loan up to 70 percent of the building's value to a strong investor. This means that $525,000 of the purchase price can be financed by someone with enough credit. So, you have to find $225,000 in cash. You have only $25,000. Suppose you brought in four investors who could put up $100,000 each, plus their share of all closing costs and points. This would work. The five of you could buy the building as a partnership.

Since you have only one-fourth of the amount of cash required of the other investors, you need something to sweeten the deal. In exchange for your lower cash investment, you agree to manage and maintain the building for the next five years without compensation for your work. This works out to a cost of $15,000 a year for the building. Divided by the four big investors, this is only $3,750. Management cost alone is often figured at ten percent of the gross rental income. Maintenance work is added to this cost. Using this template, your offer is a good one for all involved.

You will get your "own" apartment to live in, the investors will be operating under a desirable business structure, and you will be owning a full one-fifth of the property. The building doesn't become a co-op. It is still a typical apartment building, but you have created your own co-op environment, so to speak. Instead of sharing expenses with 14 residents, you will share them with four investors. This puts a bigger bite on your bank account, but you have more control and a larger equity interest. This type of approach is not for everyone, but it works out well for some people.

THE CO-OP CORPORATION

A co-op corporation owns the entire building in which cooperative units are housed. This is different from a condominium arrangement. As you learned in the previous chapter, the association controls common areas and elements. In the case of co-ops, the corporation has total ownership. As a co-op owner, you don't own any physical aspect of your dwelling unit. As a stockholder, you own a piece of the entire building, but you don't own any particular piece.

CONDO OWNERS HAVE A DEED TO THEIR AIR SPACE, CO-OP OWNERS DO NOT.

The fact that a co-op corporation owns the entire building affects your co-op fees. If you owned a condo, you would pay your own mortgage and real estate taxes. With a co-op, you pay a portion of these expenses, but instead of paying for your particular unit, you pay for a portion of the whole building. Some of the costs include principal and interest on the mortgage, real estate taxes, maintenance and repair costs, and possibly management fees. Other expenses could also be involved.

Is owning an entire building better than owning the air space inside a single unit? Many real estate professionals don't believe it is. However, if the corporation is set up properly, your portion of expenses should be fair. There will likely be some residents who pay more than you do, and there will probably be some who pay less. The percentage of your fee is determined by the amount of stock you hold in the corporation.

THE BOARD OF DIRECTORS

The board of directors for a co-op project normally operates in a manner similar to what was described for condos in the previous chapter. Board members are selected from among the residents. The board makes and enforces rules pertaining to the co-op. Since we have discussed this procedure at length in the previous chapter, I don't feel it necessary to repeat the process here. However, there is one aspect of the co-op board on which I would like to give you more information.

The board of a co-op corporation can have more power than a condo board. For example, the board may have the ability to refuse the sale of stock to certain buyers. Since they are not selling real estate, the typical real estate laws do not apply. Therefore, it is relatively easy for a co-op board to get away with discrimination. This is a touchy issue that can affect you when you are buying and when you wish to sell. Let's talk briefly about a bad situation in which you could find yourself.

Assume that you have bought into a cooperative building. You live in the apartment for a few years and then realize that you need more space. You want to sell. The corporation may have control over who you can sell to. It's not likely, but it is possible, that you may be locked into your ownership against your will. If you find ready, willing, and able buyers and the corporation will not approve them, you may not be able to

CO-OP ASSOCIATIONS HOLD MORE POWER THAN THEIR CONDO COUNTERPARTS

Co-op associations often hold more power than the associations for condos. It may seem like discrimination, but some co-op boards can refuse to allow you to sell your stock, your ownership, to specific parties. Before you commit to a co-op purchase, know your rights.

transfer your stock and ownership. Check out this aspect of co-op ownership very carefully with your lawyer.

A co-op corporation may also forbid you to sublet or rent out your dwelling unit. If you are buying as a straight investment, this could be disastrous. Even if you are buying as an owner-occupant, the tight controls a corporation can place on your decisions may be more than you are willing to accept. Keep in mind, not all co-op corporations work in the same ways. Some are more liberal than others. The bottom line is this: know what you are getting into before you get into it.

Your Voting Power

We talked about the voting procedure for condos in the last chapter. The same basic principals apply to a co-op corporation. When you buy a co-op, you will be issued voting shares. The voting power given to residents is not always equal. In fact, it is common for purchasers of more expensive units to receive more voting shares. This is a concept that some buyers have trouble accepting. And, it is an issue that can come around to haunt you down the road. Let me give you an example of these potential problems.

Let's say that you have bought into a co-op where the bylaws prohibit the use of waterbeds. You, and several of your neighbors, have grown to resent this rule. It is your intent to change the ruling. To do this, you have to file papers stating your intention. Then, you have to gather signatures from other owners to present at the next board meeting. If you are successful in obtaining a majority vote on paper, the rule will probably be altered. So, you set out to get your petition signed by as many people as possible.

As you and your neighbors go door to door in search of signatures, you find mixed reactions. Some residents are opposed to waterbeds, saying they represent a risk to the physical properties of the building, but many residents support your cause. Some want waterbeds, and others are just willing to go along with you on the basis of principal.

Your co-op building contains 100 dwelling units. Of the 100 units, residents of 55 units have agreed to support your rule change. Looks like you've got it made. You have a majority of the units signed up. What could go wrong? Well, you show up at the board meeting and submit your petition. The board takes it under advisement and renders a ruling. Your request for a rule change is denied, due to a lack of majority vote. How can this be? You had residents from 55 of 100 units on your side. It's impossible that you could have lost, right? Wrong!

When you gathered signatures, you were able to amass a majority of the dwelling units. But, the units are not given equal voting shares. When the board assessed your petition, it found that even though you had a majority of the units in tow, you did not possess a majority of the voting shares. Sorry, you lose. This, of course, is a hypothetical situation, but it does illustrate how a misconception of voting power may prove to disappoint you.

> You are issued stock and voting shares when you become a purchaser. This determines your voting power.

THE MORTGAGE LOAN

The mortgage loan a co-op corporation has on a building will generally include all aspects of the real property. There is one loan, taken out by the corporation, that all co-op owners help to pay off. There are some disadvantages to this type of approach. First of all, you have no choice in the type of loan used to acquire a building, yet you are obligated to pay your portion of it. This is unlike a condo purchase, where you seek your own financing under terms and conditions that are acceptable to you. When you buy into a co-op, you are agreeing with the financial arrangements, even though you have little, if any, say in the matter.

HOW THE MORTGAGE WORKS IN A CO-OP

When you borrow money for a co-op, you are not financing a loan for real property, you are buying stock in a corporation. Don't worry, most lenders are willing to work with this type of loan. The mortgage loan on a co-op is acquired by the corporation, and you are buying only shares of stock. You have no choice in the actual loan for the building in which you live. This is very different from buying a condo, so you should check out your comfort level in this process.

What happens if some of your neighbors can't pay their portion of the building mortgage loan? In this situation, you and your equity are put at risk. A co-op corporation depends on each shareholder to pay a fair percentage of all costs, including the principal and interest on the mortgage loan. When some residents are unable to meet their financial obligations, it puts a strain on other owners in the co-op. It's possible that the building could be lost to foreclosure or bankruptcy by the corporation. As a co-op owner, you are very dependent on your fellow shareholders.

What if Your Neighbors Can't Pay Their Fees?

Let's play a little game. Say that you are a co-op owner in a building that houses 120 apartments. Without getting into too many details, let's say that each resident is responsible for paying $600 a month in co-op fees. Now, let's say that five percent of the residents are struggling financially. They are unable to pay their fees. This means that six residents are in default. This amounts to $3,600 a month. Divided among the remaining 114 residents, this represents a cost of $31.58 that must be absorbed by the residents in good standing. This is bad, but not too bad. Suppose fifteen percent of the residents were in default. This would amount to 18 people at $600 a month, or $10,800. Your portion of this would be $105.88. See how quickly your monthly cost could rise? Someone has to make up for what others are not paying. If no one does, your home could be snatched out from under you.

A lot of potential co-op buyers are not aware of the interdependency they will share with their neighbors. You should be aware of this before you purchase stock in a co-op corporation. There are risks associated with co-ops—and condos—that don't apply to traditional detached housing. Unfortunately, there are not enough good ways to fully protect yourself when you are dealing with a community-living situation. You can, however, hedge your odds by looking into past financial statements, annual reports, property condition, and other factors that affect the success of a development.

HOW TO BUY INTO A CO-OP

There are two common ways for a person to buy into a co-op. You may go out searching for a co-op to purchase. Or, your landlord or developer may come to you and offer you an opportunity to buy shares of stock that will entitle you to live in the apartment where you presently reside. If you are an existing tenant, there is a good chance you will be offered a purchase option at below market rates. Assuming that the offer is legitimate, this is an excellent way to make a wise investment that will net you considerable equity. However, don't jump on the offer blindly. There is much you need to know before you commit to a purchase.

Before you venture into any type of deal, you should consult appropriate professionals within the field. Most commonly, this will include a CPA and an attorney when you are buying real estate. It may also include a real estate broker, a property inspector, and other professionals. I'm not suggesting that you establish your own partnership to gain the benefits of co-op living, but it is an option that you may want to consider.

Proprietary Leases

When you buy into a co-op development, you are buying stock in the co-op corporation and being issued a *proprietary lease* for the unit that you will occupy. What is a proprietary lease? It is a legal document between you and the co-op corporation that spells out the terms and conditions under which you may occupy your dwelling unit. It is not a deed to real property, such as you would get if you bought a condo.

The number of shares of stock you receive with your lease will vary, depending upon any number of circumstances. For example, some co-ops issue stock based on the square footage of your dwelling unit. The location of your unit may influence the number of shares of stock you receive. Before you buy any co-op, find out how shares are calculated and administered. The number of shares you receive affects your voting power.

Some co-op organizations don't look fondly on buyers who finance a large part of their purchase price. You may find that

INSIDER TIP

The desirability of a co-op can affect the number of shares an owner is issued in the co-op corporation. A unit with an ocean view, for example, is more valuable than a unit that looks out over the parking lot. Don't assume that all units will come with equal numbers of stock shares. Confirm what you will be getting before you make a commitment.

the corporation will require you to come up with a substantial sum of money, that is not borrowed, to buy into the corporation with full voting rights. This, to me, doesn't seem fair, but I've heard of situations where it was the case. Have your attorney review all aspects of your purchase before you sign any agreements with a seller.

ARE YOU BUYING A BUSINESS OR A HOME?

Are you buying a business or a home when you buy a co-op? Most people consider it a home purchase. From a technical point of view, you are more a business partner than you are a homeowner. Legally, you are a tenant in your apartment, not the sole owner of it. Yes, you own a small piece of it, along with the rest of the property, but you do not have a deed to your apartment.

Many banks look upon a co-op purchase as a home purchase, even though it isn't. A lot of co-op owners believe, at least to some extent, that they own their apartment. They do not. You could form your own real estate partnership and create the equivalent of a co-op purchase, in a manner of speaking. Since this idea appeals to some people, let's expand on it.

THE TAX ANGLE

The tax angle for a co-op is different from that of a condo. With a condo, you own the air space and have a deed. This entitles you to potential tax savings for the interest you pay on your mortgage. In the case of a co-op, you don't hold a deed to the property. Still, you should be entitled to potential tax savings for your portion of the interest paid on the mortgage for the building. Check this out with a qualified tax expert. As long as the property is your primary or second home, you should be entitled to some tax savings.

COSTS OF CO-OP OWNERSHIP

The rising costs of home ownership can affect any homeowner. These costs, however, affect owners of co-ops and condos in a different way. The owner of an average single-family home can put off the painting of exterior siding until money is available to pay for the project. If the siding on a condo or co-op requires painting, residents will automatically be assessed a fee for their portion of the expense. This is good for the building and the community, but it can be a hardship on individual residents.

When you buy a co-op, you must plan for rising costs. As a stockholder of the corporation, you will be paying a portion for all expenses incurred that relate to the property. This can include, but is not limited to, security, lawn care, general maintenance, management, capital repairs, and improvements. If you buy a detached home that is not located in a subdivision where an association rules, you can count on a defined amount to be your primary house payment, assuming that you have a fixed-rate mortgage. Even so, certain expenses are likely to escalate over time. Your real estate taxes may go up. Utility bills tend to increase, and maintenance costs go hand in hand with home ownership. The big difference between owning a co-op or condo and a detached home, that is outside of an association, is the amount of choice you have in determining when to spend money for needed services.

The cost of maintenance, repairs, and other building requirements can rise quickly. If you are unprepared to pay your portion of the expenses, you can quickly find yourself in deep trouble. There is a possibility that you could lose your ownership interest in a co-op if you are unable to pay the fees assessed to you. It may be possible for the corporation to evict you as a tenant and sublet your dwelling unit until a new buyer is found for what was your corporate stock. If this possibility exists in the agreements you sign, you are at high risk. Make sure that your lawyer investigates this area of ownership thoroughly. This potential problem is severe enough to warrant more discussion.

Assume that you have purchased stock in a co-op corporation. You have owned it for several years. All of a sudden, you are disabled in an auto accident. Your income is cut off. Then, you get a bill for your co-op fee. You can't pay it. This goes on for three months. All of a sudden, you are served with eviction papers. Now, you are not only disabled, you have no place to live. On top of all this, you are told that your unit will be leased to someone else until a suitable buyer for your stock can be found. Your investment, your home, and your very future are at stake.

This is a serious situation, and it may be lurking somewhere in the fine print of your purchase agreement. Be absolutely certain of what you are signing before you sign it. In general, co-ops operate in a manner consistent with condos in many regards. There are, as you have seen, substantial differences between the two concepts. Chapter 6, "Condos Versus Co-ops: Pros and Cons," will show you many of the positives and negatives for each type of living space. Before you get to that stage, however, turn to the next chapter, which explores the tax and legal issues that affect each type of ownership.

CHAPTER 4

Taxes and Legal Issues

The purchase and ownership of any home involves taxes and legal issues. This is the case whether you buy a condo, a co-op, or a detached home. A real estate transaction can be a complicated affair. There might be many pitfalls waiting for you as you attempt to buy a new home. If you are working with a good buyer's broker, you can avoid most of the traps. But, there comes a time when the assistance of a real estate broker is not enough. Unless you are an expert in these fields, you should seek competent council from tax and legal experts. There is no suitable substitute for CPAs and attorneys when it comes to questions on taxes and legal issues. Without this type of aid, you can find yourself in a lot of trouble

This chapter covers many of the legal and tax issues that may affect you as a purchaser of a condo or co-op. For example, what portion of your home ownership is tax deductible? Is a lawyer needed to complete your transaction? How serious and how restrictive are the rules which may pertain to your home ownership? These questions, and many more, will be answered in this chapter.

TAX ISSUES

Most prospective home buyers have heard a lot about the tax advantages of owning real estate. Are the deductions real? Can owning your own home really cost about the same, or even less than renting? The answer to both questions is a resounding Yes! There are many potential tax advantages associated with home ownership. Tax consequences and tax questions should be top issues for anyone buying a home to consider. The following information will lead you through the maze of questions and advantages pertaining to the tax angles of buying a home of your own.

- Are there homeowner tax advantages?
- How do you assess your tax consequences?
- What other tax questions should you ask?

Tax Advantages

You've probably heard about all the tax advantages that homeowners get. This might even be a motivating factor in your decision to buy a home. The potential tax savings are reason enough to want to own a home of your own, but you never know when the tax laws will be changed. What is a valid deduction this year might not be valid next year. Don't depend on the assumption that current tax advantages will always be available. In all probability, homeowner tax advantages will stay with us for many years to come, but we can't count on this.

Are there tax advantages worth consideration for people who own their own homes? Absolutely. Most homeowners can save a substantial amount of money on their income taxes by taking allowable homeowner deductions. Real estate taxes and the interest paid on a home mortgage are both deductible expenses in most cases. It's not difficult for the savings to equal more than $300 a month. This, depending upon your point of view, is in effect lowering the cost of a mortgage payment by $300 a month. This type of savings can make a mortgage payment cost less than rent once the tax savings are realized.

Tax Consequences

Tax consequences have to be assessed on an individual basis. What works for one person does not work for all people. Before you make any assumptions, talk to qualified experts in your area for current and complete data on both tax and legal issues. I am not a CPA or an attorney. My experience is as a broker and investor. However, I do consult with both lawyers and CPAs frequently to stay abreast of what's going on in their fields pertaining to real estate. Use the information in this chapter as a source of knowledge and a way of learning what questions to ask. Don't take the material out of context. I am offering neither tax nor legal advice. My effort is only to inform you of my personal experiences and to give you information that may help you when you talk with local professionals.

Tax Questions

You might not have many tax questions to ask an accountant. Even if this is the case, you should talk with a tax expert about the purchase of your new home. If you don't take advantage of the tax savings that are rightfully yours, you are losing a lot of money for nothing. Your personal tax bracket, income sources, and home will have an affect on what your personal tax advantages will be. Until you talk with an expert about your specific circumstances, you can't be absolutely sure of what your tax situation will be once you become a homeowner. The following list presents some possible questions you may wish to ask:

- What sort of tax breaks will you receive?
- How do you determine your tax savings?
- Can you deduct your association fees?

Condo Tax Breaks Versus Co-op Tax Breaks

Are you going to buy a condo or a co-op? Condo owners get tax breaks in the same way that owners of detached homes do. The rules are different for co-op owners. Both types of property can afford you some tax savings, but the process differs. Under general conditions, a condo owner can write off all property taxes and mortgage interest paid on the condo. Co-op owners get their deductions based on the percentage of taxes and interest that they pay on their building. How Do You Determine Your Tax Savings?

To how much will the tax savings really amount? You will have to talk to a local professional to determine your personal savings. I can, however, show you an example that might apply to you. Let's say that you are in the 28 percent tax bracket. Plus, you pay a 6 percent state tax. The total tax bite is 34 percent. Now let's assume that your total annual expense for mortgage interest and real estate taxes is $14,000. With the typical tax advantages, you will reduce your taxes by $4,760, which is a savings of nearly $400 a month. Now, let's carry this information into another situation.

Let's say that you own a condo and pay $1,166.67 per month for your mortgage payment and real estate taxes. Let's say that the condo is a converted apartment. Similar apartments, that aren't as nice, are renting for $750 a month. Well, buying your own condo is going to cost you a lot more than renting, isn't it? Not really, factor in your tax savings. When you deduct your $400 savings each month from your housing cost, you are paying $766.67 for your condo. This is less than twenty dollars more than what you would pay in rent for a lesser unit. Granted, you have to make the higher payments and recoup your savings at tax time, but if you can do this, buying is a big advantage.

Can You Take Fee Deductions?

Can you deduct the cost of your association fee? Not likely. Check with your accountant, but I don't think you will be able to. Are maintenance expenses deductible for you? Again, it's doubtful. If you were an absentee owner, you could probably get some mileage out of maintenance costs, but as an owner-occupant it is not likely. The best advice I can give you on your tax savings is to talk to a CPA who understands the workings of condos and co-ops. You may need some paperwork that details your requirements for expenses to help your CPA make a fair judgment. If you have a copy of your building's bylaws and rules, bring them with you to the tax meeting.

LEGAL ISSUES

Do you need a lawyer when you buy a condo or co-op? Technically, you don't have to engage a lawyer for advice, but you should. Transactions in real estate can involve a variety of legal issues that the average person doesn't understand. Hey, some lawyers don't understand them, and this is a fact that you should keep in mind. Not all attorneys deal in real estate. You want one who does. Preferably, you want a lawyer who has a lot of experience in condos and co-ops, if that's what you are buying.

Most people recognize the need for professional guidance when entering into a contract to purchase a home. However, it surprises me how many people don't seek approval from an attorney before making one of the biggest commitments of their lives. A vast number of home buyers rely almost solely on their real estate broker in contract matters. Many brokers are very astute on the legal issues of real estate and contracts, but they are not lawyers. Brokers are best known for selling real estate, not for interpreting legal issues. A broker can be a big help to you when going to contract on a property, but I believe you should consult with your attorney before putting your pen to the paper.

Lawyers often charge large hourly rates. You could easily pay over $100 an hour for the advice you receive from your legal expert. Since a broker might help you for free, what would induce you to pay large fees out of your own pocket? Well, how much is the property that you are buying going to cost? If you're buying a unit that costs $150,000, a few hundred dollars in legal fees doesn't seem so large. I must stress to you, real estate deals can be filled with hooks and problems. While most deals are made without incident, there is always the possibility that things could turn very bad. What you save by not talking with an attorney could be lost very quickly with just one wrong move. To expound on this, let's look at a few scenarios in which having a lawyer in your corner is a valuable investment.

Legal Issues

- What do you know about association agreements?
- Do you know exactly what you are buying?
- Are there back taxes or liens on the property you are buying?
- Have you received a full disclosure on the property?
- Is your contract both legal and enforceable?
- Are you working with a boiler-plate contract?
- Is there a "time is of the essence" clause in your contract?
- What are the contingency clauses in your contract?
- Have you established a time of acceptance for your offer?

- How much of a deposit are you making in your purchase?
- Can you get your deposit back if the deal goes bad?
- How much will brokerage fees amount to?
- Do you understand closing costs and points?
- When will possession be granted to you?

What Is in Your Association Agreement?

When you buy into a development that has an association with bylaws and rules, you expose yourself to additional risk. People who have a custom home built don't normally have to deal with bylaws and rules that are put in place by a board of directors. Condo and co-op buyers have more legal considerations to review. This is a job for your attorney.

Can you live with a condo where you are not allowed to have pets on the premises? Does it bother you that your co-op organization can prevent you from selling your unit to specific buyers? Issues such as these come up from time to time. You may not be able to use your unit as rental property if you decide to move. Maybe you won't be allowed to park your recreational vehicle on the property. There can be a wide variety of rules and regulations to abide by when you buy a condo or co-op. To be safe, you need your attorney to dissect the paperwork provided to you. Then, have the attorney explain each and every rule, regulation, and condition to your satisfaction. Failure to do this could result in a very unhappy purchasing experience.

Do You Know What You Are Buying?

I've heard of cases in which buyers thought they were buying one property, when they were, in fact, buying a different property. You, your broker, or your attorney should confirm that the legal description provided in your contract is the description of the property that you are buying. It's a wise idea to request a copy of the deed when buying any type of property. You're probably starting to see how acting as your own representative could be risky. This is why I recommend the use of a lawyer in all real estate deals.

Are There Back Taxes and Liens?

Back taxes and liens, both those filed and those that may be filed, are concerns in a real estate transaction. If property taxes have not been paid on a property that you are buying, you could wind up in a world of financial trouble. Require a guarantee, and preferably proof, that all taxes are paid up to date and have a pro-ration agreement in your contract for any fuel expenses, taxes, or other costs that might be associated with your sale.

Have You Received Full Disclosures?

Full disclosures are generally given in real estate transactions. The disclosures can deal with lead paint, septic systems, the quality of drinking water, insulation, asbestos, and other items of interest. If you are not provided with a disclosure statement, you should ask for one. The disclosure should be given to you prior to you making an offer to purchase. Most brokers are good about this, but you might run into a situation with a seller where a disclosure is not offered. If this is the case, beware! Talk to your attorney for advice on how to proceed if you don't receive a satisfactory disclosure sheet.

Is Your Contract Legal and Enforceable?

Oral contracts are legal, but not enforceable. This means, for the most part, that they are worthless. Require all terms of your purchase to be in writing. There is no exception here. You can listen to what brokers say and you can hear the statements of sellers, but depend only on what you have in black and white. If it's not addressed in your contract, you are out of luck in a court battle.

It's usually little issues that fester in oral agreements. For example, a seller might tell you that the drapes come with the condo. You assume this true, so you don't think to specify it in your contract. After you close on your deal, you find that the drapes are gone. Can you go after the seller? You can sue them, but the odds of you winning in court are nearly nonexistent. The question of *chattel* (personal property) comes up often in verbal exchanges. Does the free-standing fireplace go with the home? Will the seller be leaving the washer and dryer? Do you get the refrigerator and range in the kitchen? Items like these are not real property. They don't have to convey with a sale. If you want something that is questionable, put your request in the contract. Stipulate that all appliances convey to you. This way, you are protected with legal rights of enforcement.

Do You Have a Boiler-Plate Contract?

It is quite common for brokers to use boiler-plate, fill-in-the-blank contracts. Most of the agreements are acceptable, subject to what is placed in the blanks. However, you should have your attorney review the contracts very carefully. Any time that you get a legal document from someone who is not representing you, you have to be on the lookout for problems. Even if the document is coming from someone in your camp, you should read it thoroughly. Fill-in-the-blank contracts typically contain standard provisions for basic contract requirements. Most of the concern comes from what is written into the blank areas.

Skillful brokers and attorneys can use specific words to slant a contract to the advantage of their client. As a typical citizen, you might not notice what the words mean. This can be a big mistake. Unless you are absolutely certain of what you are reading, don't agree to the terms. Once you sign a real estate contract, you are probably going to have to live with it. The chances of revoking your signature are not good.

Time Is of the Essence Clauses

When you see the words "time is of the essence" does it mean anything to you? It should if you are buying a home. Basically, this one little phrase can cost you your earnest-money deposit and your ability to buy a property that you have under contract. When a purchase contract contains a time-is-of-the-essence clause, you must close your deal by the date described, or the seller has a right to keep your deposit and void your deal. Most brokers know this, and they should tell you about it, but they might not. Your lawyer will probably advise you not to accept a contract with this type of language in it. You don't have control of your mortgage company and the other elements that might prolong your closing. Someone else's mistake could cost you a lot of money and the opportunity to acquire the home of your dreams, and it's all possible with just five little words.

Contingency Clauses

Contingency clauses are common elements in real estate contracts. These clauses allow you to tie up a property while you obtain answers to various questions you might have about the property. For example, if you want to have a professional property inspection performed on a building, you could use a contingency clause to get the unit you want to buy off the open market while you are having the inspection done. Contingency clauses can be used for just about any question you may have.

The clauses are a powerful tool for you as a buyer. A good real estate lawyer can advise you what clauses are appropriate and needed to protect your purchase.

Won't my broker instruct me in the use of contingency clauses? A buyer's broker should, but a seller's broker is required to make the best deal possible for a seller, and this may mean not giving you any unsolicited advice on contingency clauses. The clauses are not as good for sellers as they are for buyers. Brokers you ask about contingency clauses should answer you honestly, but don't expect seller's brokers to offer you such advice unless you ask specific questions. An attorney, however, is working for you and should be looking out for your best interest.

What Is Your Time for Acceptance?

When you make a purchase offer, you should include a time for acceptance by which the seller must abide. Otherwise, you have a live offer laying around for as long as the seller chooses to keep it. This will prevent you from placing an offer on another property. Some buyers give sellers 24 hours to accept, counter, or reject an offer. It's not uncommon for a seller to have three days for acceptance. The key is to limit the length of time that a seller has to sit on your offer. You need this protection. A broker working in your behalf should take care of this, but make sure that you don't sign an offer that doesn't have an expiration date.

How Much of a Deposit Do You Have to Put Down?

How much of a deposit do you have to put with a purchase offer? Basically, you have to provide a deposit that is acceptable to the seller. There is no set figure that is needed to make a contract legal or enforceable. It is my understanding that no money has to change hands. I've been told the consideration must be given, but this can be a promise for a promise, not necessarily cash. Monetary deposits are the typical type of deposit used, but they don't have to be large. I've sealed many deals, both as a buyer and a broker, with only $100 as a deposit. It is to your advantage to keep your deposit as small as possible.

Who's going to have control of your deposit money? When a listing broker is involved, the agency that holds the property listing typically keeps deposits in an escrow account. This does not have to be the case, as long as all parties to a contract agree on the terms. If you are using a buyer's broker, you could request that your broker hold the deposit. An attorney could also be designated to hold a deposit; this would be the best bet if brokers are not involved in a transaction. It's risky to allow a seller to hold a deposit.

There is one advantage to including a large deposit with your purchase offer. If you offer a substantial deposit, sellers may take your offer more seriously. My experience, however, has proved that this is rarely something about which a buyer has to worry. Talk to your broker and attorney for specific advice, but under average conditions, I would keep my contract deposit no more than $500.

Will You Get Your Deposit Back?

Will I get my deposit back if my financing is not approved? It depends on the wording in your contract. Most real estate contracts contain provisions for deposits to revert back to buyers if the buyers are turned down for financing. Don't assume this will be the case in your situation. The terms and conditions surrounding your deposit should be spelled out in clear language. Personally, I would not enter into a purchase agreement without a contingency for financing approval. Again, your broker or lawyer can advise you on this issue.

Do You Pay Brokerage Fees?

Your contract should state which party is paying brokerage fees. Traditionally, sellers have paid brokerage fees. Since buyer's brokers have become popular, the payment of fees has shifted to some extent. It is not unusual for a buyer to pay a buyer's broker directly and to ask for a lower sales price because of the payment. Neither is it uncommon for sellers to pay a fee that will be provided to a buyer's broker. The point is this, you need to know who is paying the brokerage fees. Have the terms of payment detailed in your sales contract.

What are Your Closing Costs and Points?

Who is going to pay what when it comes to closing costs and points? This is another issue that should be spelled out in your purchase agreement. Will the seller be paying a portion of your expenses? It's common for buyers and sellers to pay only their own portion of closing costs and points. There is no rule, however, that says you can't negotiate different payment terms. It's not rare to find sellers paying some of the closing costs and points for buyers. In some types of financing, sellers are required to pay points. All of this needs to be spelled out in a contract to purchase real estate.

When Will You Take Possession?

When will you obtain possession of your unit? Possession is normally given at the time of closing, but again, this is a negotiable issue. Maybe you will get possession as soon as your loan is approved. The seller may want to retain possession for two weeks after closing, to make arrangements for moving. There is no surefire standard to this issue. It's natural to assume that you will have possession at the time of closing, but don't make assumptions in a real estate deal. Put everything in writing, and don't leave any questions unanswered.

BUYING A UNIT THAT DOES NOT YET EXIST

Buying a unit that does not yet exist gives you a chance for some quick equity gain, but it can also set the stage for disastrous results. How much money are you going to have to put up for a property on paper? What guarantee do you have that the builder or developer will not go bankrupt? Is a performance bond in place? What will happen if the developer doesn't build the entire development? When you are buying into a new project, you have a lot more questions to have answered. This is true of both new construction and conversion projects.

Developers and their sales associates can make promises that seem too good to be true. Sometimes they are too good to be true. A lot of people do buy units before they exist, and most of the projects work out. But, you can't afford to be caught up in one that doesn't work. Different states have varying laws pertaining to selling homes from blueprints. Your attorney can be your best friend when you are buying what some people refer to as a "paper home." You need someone who can cut through the hype and see the project for what it will really be. Under the right conditions, buying a unit before it is built or converted can be quite profitable.

How do you feel about retaining the services of an attorney? Hopefully, you've seen enough of the potential pitfalls to recognize the value of an experienced lawyer. Talk with a CPA and a lawyer before you get too far into your purchase of a home. The initial consultations may be free, and you can't beat a price like that. Even if you have to shell out a couple hundred dollars, it may be the best money you will ever spend. Seriously, you should work with expert professionals when you are dealing in

CAN THEY DELIVER ON THEIR PROMISES?

Over the years, I have seen a lot of advertising that was hard to believe. I've heard builders and developers present sales seminars with promises that were almost impossible to perform. It is often said that salespeople will tell prospective buyers whatever they want to hear The following are just some examples of what you might be promised, but never see:

> "Oh sure, of course there's going to be a swimming pool. It's going to be right over there, just as soon as we get approval for it."
>
> "How long will it take us to complete your unit? Oh, we can have you in there in less than a month."
>
> "If you buy right now, you can have a free dishwasher." (This is when the dishwasher is already a planned amenity.)
>
> "The jets really don't come over this site very often."
>
> "Can you have pets? Well, I'm pretty sure that you can; in fact, I can hardly imagine that you can't."

I have terminated sales associates for promising customers the moon. There have been a few people who sold my units who would be selling during construction and basically paint a total fantasy picture in the mind of the buyers. This is bad for the customer, and it's bad for the builder who has to deal with the disgruntled customer who was promised more than what was really being offered. To protect yourself from such actions, get all the promises in writing.

real estate. The industry is not a place for the inexperienced. Now, let's move on to the next chapter and talk about common space, repairs, and restrictions.

Chapter 5

Common Space, Repairs and Restrictions

When it comes to common space, repairs, and restrictions, many condo and co-op owners don't understand the procedures that apply to their units. It's not really difficult to sort through the responsibilities expected of owners, yet many owners never take the time to become familiar with their community rules. Sometimes, owners find out the hard way what they can and can't do. This can be a costly lesson.

Some people, especially those who buy into cooperative apartments, feel that life will go on as it did before the building became a co-op. This is especially true of buyers who were tenants in the building prior to the co-op conversion. People who lived in apartments often expect routine maintenance to be done by a maintenance person employed by the apartment building. The confusion, related to maintenance, that can be created in a co-op project has the potential to create angry residents.

What is common space? Who's responsible for the upkeep of this space? Do you have to pay for work done in common areas? These are just a few of the questions that may come up when you buy a condo or co-op. Does the co-op association have to make repairs to appliances in your apartment? Who determines if you can have a pet? The questions pertaining to repairs and restrictions can be difficult to answer. You can, however, take the mystery out of these questions by seeking answers in the right places. This chapter is a good place to start.

BEFORE YOU BUY

Before you buy a condo or a co-op, you need to research all aspects of your purchase. Part of this research should include a full review of the organization's bylaws, rules, regulations, and deed restrictions. As a prospective purchaser, you have a right to see what you are buying into. Many slick-talking salespeople will fly right over the subjects that you should know the most about. The sales associates may be fast to point out the high-tech dishwasher, the large bathroom, and the cheerful living room. But, people who are trying to make a sale might do little more than casually mention that you will have to abide by community regulations once you become an owner.

If you ask to see a copy of the association's bylaws, you should be given the opportunity. Some salespeople may try to hedge on this request. They may tell you that only owners have access to the bylaws. Don't you believe it. If you have to, have your attorney draw up an offer to purchase that is subject to your satisfactory review of all applicable restrictions, rules, and regulations. This will show the seller that you are serious about buying, but that you won't make a final commitment until you've read all of the documentation pertaining to you and your prospective unit.

Unless you are an expert in real estate, you should definitely have an attorney go over all the paperwork with you. Even if you are a real estate pro, it's a good idea to get a second opinion from an attorney. It's scary to think of all the trouble you could be buying into with a condo or co-op. For that matter, any real estate purchase can be loaded with negative points that could have an adverse affect on you.

COMMON SPACE

Common space is one of the easiest aspects of condo and co-op ownership to understand. If you don't own it, but are allowed to use it, it's *common space*. This simplifies the situation to an extreme, but it is an accurate description of common space. We will go into more detail on both common space and common elements later in this chapter.

INSIDER TIPS

Common space is space to which anyone living in a condo or co-op community has access, such as a swimming pool or tennis court. A common element is something that affects the overall development but is restricted to the use of only the individual property owner. Decks and balconies are examples of common elements.

Condo and co-op developments both have some common space. Some developments have more than others. As an owner, you pay for this space indirectly. The dues you pay your association are used to create, operate, and maintain common space and common elements. Some common space is easy to identify. Other types of common space and common elements are not so easy to tag. For example, is the deck behind your condo yours, or is it common space? People from the next building are not provided with any rights to come and use your deck. So, it must be private, right? Don't count on it. The deck is probably considered a common element. What, you don't even own your own deck? Maybe not. This is the way confusion sets in, so let's clarify the situation.

The following paragraphs show many scenarios pertaining to common space and common elements. Since we started with a deck as an example, let's stick with it for a few more minutes. How can you own a condo and not own the deck that is attached to it? In most condos, the owner has full possession of the air space within the condo. We've talked about this before. If the air space is your only ownership interest, the deck would be considered a common element. And, this is almost always how it works with a condo.

Co-ops and condos are very similar in their allocation of common space. A co-op owner is only the owner of stock. The owner has no full ownership of the co-op building, its units, its grounds, or its amenities. Co-op owners hold leases that give them exclusive use of some part of the co-op. The part normally given for exclusive use is an apartment. Any part of the co-op that is outside of the apartment is generally treated as common space.

Many people have no trouble determining what belongs to them and what is common space. Other people become confused when they find out that they don't own their deck or balcony. It can be even more confusing to find out that you don't own the siding or the roofing that covers the exterior of your home. Co-op owners tend to be more in touch with the common-space issue than condo owners. This may be because condos give an impression of more traditional real estate ownership.

TYPES OF COMMON SPACE

There are many types of common space. Most of them are easy to identify. Who owns the playground that your children use? The association controls it. Is the parking lot common space? It is, but you may be offered reserved parking in it. This doesn't mean that you own your parking spaces, but you are entitled to exclusive use of them. If your community has swimming pools or tennis courts, they are considered common space. Walking trails are another example of common space.

Figuring out that a swimming pool is common space is not difficult. It makes sense. But, does the fact that the sidewalk up to your front door is not owned by you make sense? Maybe not, but you don't own anything outside of your living unit in most condo and co-op developments. Certainly you must own your own front door! Not likely. The front door of a condo or co-op is usually considered association property. You have the right to paint the interior portion of the door, but you can't replace the door with one of a different type, without board approval.

Imagine buying a home and not owning the front door. It's hard to envision, isn't it? Well, there are plenty of other situations that may be more difficult to believe. Who owns the shrubs that grow in front of your condo? It's not you. The association controls the plants. Keep in mind, there are exceptions to what I'm saying. A development can set up its own rules and regulations in any legal way. You might own your own plants, but you can count on the fact that they must be of an approved type and maintained properly.

Do you own the grass that surrounds your condo? No, you don't. Can the neighborhood kids use your lawn for soccer practice? No. You have the exclusive use of your lawn. Are you tired of looking at the same old light fixture by your front door on a daily basis? Hey, why not replace it with a pretty, brass fixture? You'd better get board approval first, because the light doesn't belong to you.

Read the Fine Print

It's easy to see why some people don't understand the limits of common space and common elements. Many salespeople don't point out all the little ownership details to perspective purchasers. If the sales associates make any mention of this subject, it's usually fast and buried under some type of sales hype. Are the salespeople misleading you? Probably not. Real estate laws are generally strict, and full disclosure is required of a seller. This disclosure, however, can take many shapes. If you are handed a thick package of brochures and paperwork, you might never dig through it to find the restrictions pertaining to the community. You've been give the information, so the salespeople are not violating any laws. But, did you see and understand all of what you were given? Maybe, maybe not, but that's your responsibility.

It is standard procedure in both condos and co-ops for the association to be in charge of all exterior items and elements. The control of the association is not limited to exterior space. Hallways are common space when they exist outside of your dwelling units. The physical walls, floors, and ceilings are controlled by an association. The truth is, you don't have exclusive use or ownership of much when you buy a condo or co-op.

WHO PAYS FOR COMMON-SPACE MAINTENANCE?

Who pays for maintenance and repairs to common space? In most cases, all homeowners pay a portion of this expense. The board of directors for a development allocates the funds, and individual property owners provide the funds. The collection of money for maintenance and repairs is done through regular association dues. In some cases, a special assessment is made on homeowners to cover the cost of large or unexpected repairs and replacements. Since we covered this type of information in previous chapters, let's shift our focus to what you pay for directly.

You already know that you pay a portion for all expenses related to what the association does for you. Examples of this type of service could include grass cutting, exterior painting, landscaping, snow removal, and so forth. Once buyers understand what common space is, they can usually accept when and how they pay for it. Most of the questions raised around the issue of repairs have to do with in-building problems.

THEIR REPAIRS OR YOURS?

Let's say that you live in a co-op. You come home late one evening and discover that the elevator is out of order. Are you going to call a repair company to come fix the elevator? I seriously doubt it. You will probably call the management company or your association to report the failure. This is something of a no-brainer. But, what if the light bulb is burned out in the fixture at your front door? Are you going to replace it, or are you going to call for association maintenance? Most people would replace the light bulb. It's simply faster and easier to do this than it is to call for maintenance. Technically, you may not have a right to replace the light bulb. However, you will probably be responsible for keeping the light working. Are you confused yet?

CONSUMABLES

You know, from reading your development's bylaws, that you cannot alter the exterior light fixture in any way without board approval. The light is considered a common element. So, when the bulb burns out, shouldn't the association pay to have it replaced? It depends on the structure of your association. You might find that you are required to pay for *consumables*, such as light bulbs, and that the association will take care of structural repairs and replacements. In other words, you are responsible for keeping light bulbs in the light. But, if a vandal breaks the light fixture, the association will repair or replace it, at no direct cost to you. This is what can make repairs so confusing.

Who has to replace the door handle on your front door if it fails to operate properly? It may be your responsibility, or the task may fall on the shoulders of the association. If you are required to make the replacement, you can bet that the new hardware will have to comply with association guidelines.

Whose Insurance Pays for Damages?

When you bought your co-op, it came with a fully-equipped kitchen. The dishwasher has now sprung a leak and ruined the ceiling in the apartment below you. Is this your problem, or will the co-op be responsible for the damage? More than likely, you will be held responsible for all aspects of the damage. You should have insurance that will protect you from the costs, but don't expect the association to bail you out. You might think that since you are a lessee in your apartment that the co-op is responsible for damages of this type. This line of thinking is rarely, if ever, correct.

Now, let's look at a different type of example. Assume that you bought a condo a few years ago. The bathroom in the condo looked good when you bought it, but the floor squeaked a little, around the toilet. The problem has grown worse, and the floor feels spongy when you walk on it. You call in a contractor who tells you that the sub-flooring has rotted, due to a leak around the base of the toilet. You own the toilet and the floor covering, but the development owns the sub-flooring and the floor joists. Who's going to pay? An insurance company is probably going to pay for the repairs. If you split hairs, you would be responsible for the floor covering and plumbing expenses, while the association would have to take care of the structural damage. Again, each development can have different rules, so you have to know exactly what you are dealing with to be safe.

Do You Need Board Approval?

- *Do you need board approval to replace the kitchen countertop in your condo?* No.
- *Can you change the light fixture on the exterior of your condo?* Yes, but you have to make sure the replacement is in compliance with your association rules.

- *Can the condo association dictate to you what color your siding may be?* Absolutely, anything to do with the exterior of your unit will come under association scrutiny.
- *Who is responsible if your refrigerator, that came with your condo, goes on the blink?* You are. Interior maintenance and repair falls upon your shoulders.
- *How do you obtain board or association approval?* You will normally have to go to a meeting and petition the organization for permission to achieve your goal.

Interior Versus Exterior Painting

Who is responsible for the cost when your condo or co-op needs to be painted? Ah, we don't yet have enough information to answer the question. Is the painting taking place outside or inside? Inside painting is the financial responsibility of the resident. Exterior painting is generally done by the association. Do you have any say in what color paint is used for the painting? Inside your unit, you have complete control over the color scheme. This will not be the case with exterior painting. You may have to maintain a color that matches, as nearly as possible, with your original paint color. Or, you may be given a choice among several colors that are acceptable to the association. You will not, however, have a free hand to pick any color you like for the exterior painting.

Window Repairs

Windows can be an interesting topic when it comes to repairs and replacements. Let's say that your heating and cooling expenses are higher than you would like for them to be. It is your belief that cheap windows are a contributor to your problem. Can you call up one of the quick-fix, home-improvement companies that pitches super-insulated windows to have your home fitted with new, energy-efficient windows? You can call the company, but you had better get board approval before you alter your existing windows.

Who owns your windows? You may own the interior section of the window, but your development probably owns the exterior. Will the board of directors for your association allow you to upgrade your windows with new ones? Probably, but the board is likely to require your new windows to be of a style that is complimentary to the community. See how easy it is to have your hands tied on repairs and improvements? Most associations and boards of directors are reasonable with the residents that they serve. No organization wants to have disgruntled residents in their buildings. But, don't expect the board members to cower to your every request. It can, in fact, be very difficult to get board approval for repairs and improvements that meet your personal criteria.

Structural Maintenance Versus Modification

If you are living in a co-op and the laminate on your kitchen counter begins to bubble, buckle, and peel up, who is going to fix it? This is a situation where you are responsible for seeing that the repair is made. The co-op has no interest in your countertop. But, suppose you decide that you don't want so much counter space. Maybe you want to do away with the "L" shape and have just a short counter, so that you can open up the eat-in area of your kitchen. Can you do this? Of course you can, but you might be violating the terms of your purchase agreement or lease if you do.

The counter in your co-op exists for your personal and exclusive use. However, your lease or purchase agreement probably prohibits you from altering the structural size, shape, and condition of the counter. Ripping out the counter for more space could put you in deep trouble. If the co-op ever exercised its right to reclaim your unit, you might be held liable for your actions with the counter. I know this may seem strange and unfair, but it could be the way things occur.

How can it be fair that you, the person who is paying the bills, can't alter your kitchen counter? Well, if the co-op has to repossess your unit, the unit should be in a condition that is consistent with what it was when you purchased it. Putting a new top on the counter would be fine. You have complete discretion as to this. But, tearing part of the counter out is more radical, and this could be a violation of your agreement with the co-op association. You may resent the restraints that apply to you as a co-op or condo owner, but you must recognize that this type of living is different from independent, detached-home life.

Your Options

Your options for repairs and replacements as the owner of a condo or co-op can be quite limited. This is not always the case, but it can prove to be true. Condo owners and co-op owners have a different form of ownership from each other. As a condo owner, you own the floor coverings, wall coverings, ceiling coverings, and all of the basic fixtures, cabinets, and decorations within your personal unit.

Co-op owners own only stock. The lease given to a co-op buyer authorizes certain and specific aspects of co-op living. Since every development can make its own rules, it's difficult to say exactly what a co-op owner has a right to do. Can you replace your carpet? Probably. Is it okay for you to get rid of pink plumbing fixtures and replace them with almond-colored fixtures? Most likely. However, you must read and understand all of the rules by which you must abide before you make repairs and replacements. This is a very difficult duty for some buyers to accept.

I live in a single-family, detached home on 25 acres of land. The house was designed by me and my wife, and we built it. There is a mortgage on the home that limits us, to a small extent, on what we can and can't do. Otherwise, we can do anything we want to with the property. If I want to paint the siding on my house in a fluorescent orange color, I can. Condo and co-op owners don't have this freedom. Should I decide to house six dogs in my garage, I can. This would not be the case with many co-op or condo owners. There is, without doubt, much more freedom for homeowners who do not live by association rules. Even so, the trade-offs for community living can out weigh the freedom of complete independence. When my roof needs to be replaced, I will have to pay the full price. If I lived in a condo or a co-op, I would be paying only a portion of the expense. There are pros and cons to all forms of habitation.

If you have a personality of a free spirit, you could find yourself at either end of the spectrum with community living. My connotation of a free spirit is having control over my own actions and life. This encourages me to live in a detached home that is not controlled by an association. However, if your idea of being free is to never have to cut your grass or paint your siding, community living in a condo or co-op should make you happy. Each person has to find a balance point to be comfortable.

Special Assessments

Special assessments for major repairs and replacements may be one of the largest risks that you will assume as an owner of a condo or co-op. In reality, this risk is not much greater than it would be if you owned your own, detached home in a rural location. If my roof needs to be replaced, I have to pay for all the labor and material to do it. As an owner of a condo or co-op, I'd pay only a portion of the cost. The roof would be larger, so the cost would be greater. Yet, the expense would be spread out among the other residents, so my out-of-pocket expense would probably be less. Which is better? It depends on your perspective.

Would I ever live in a co-op? I would prefer not to, but this is due to my personal desires. A condo would be more agreeable with me, but I like space. Even a townhouse or a detached home in a subdivision is more restrictive than what I enjoy. My style of living calls for land and a private setting. Many people would feel uncomfortable where I live. My closest neighbor is a bull moose that roams the back yard. It's possible for my children to play safely without fear of traffic or abduction, but medical services are a full 30 minutes away. Any way you cut it, trade-offs play a large role in the lifestyle we choose.

Special assessments can amount to a lot of money. If you don't have the cash for such an expense set aside, you may have to borrow it. Owners who do not have the ability to borrow large sums can be in danger of losing their homes. This is especially true with co-op owners. Typically, co-ops have more power to remove you from your domicile than condo associations do.

What types of expenses might be levied against you in the form of special assessments? Roofing work is one possibility. Siding repairs and replacements are another. Adding or repairing a tennis court, swimming pool, or playground might call for you to cough up some cash. Foundation faults could be at the root of a special assessment. Failures of major items can account for special assessments. Are you in a position to cover your percentage of the costs? If you are not, you are at risk. Before you buy a condo or a co-op, get a clear definition of what your obligations may be during a special assessment. Failure to do this could result in the loss of your home and equity.

FREQUENTLY ENCOUNTERED RESTRICTIONS

How would it make you feel to have supreme power? Probably pretty good. Well, developers do, in a way, have supreme power. When a project is being established, the developer can create just about any rule imaginable, with the exception of something that would be considered discriminatory. For this reason, you have to investigate all restrictions very carefully. Most condo and co-op associations have reasonable restrictions, but this does not mean that they will always be suitable for you. What is an advantage to one buyer can be a disadvantage to another. You owe it to yourself to delve deeply into all aspects of your home purchase before you make your final move.

The restrictions that you may encounter from development to development may be as varied as the developments themselves. One place allow pets while another place does not. Some developments allow you to park a motorhome in the parking lot while others do not. Failure to know and understand the restrictions of a development that you are buying into can result in tremendous personal frustration. Since restrictions are at the discretion of developers and associations, there is no way that I can prepare you for all of what you might find. I can, however, give you some solid examples of what to look out for. Let's do this now.

SOME COMMON RESTRICTIONS THAT MAY AFFECT YOU

- Some associations will not allow recreational vehicles to be parked in primary parking areas. You may have to keep your RV in a compound that is designated specifically for this purpose.
- If you drive a commercial vehicle, like a plumbing van or a delivery truck, you may be prohibited from

parking it near your condo or co-op. This may seem unfair, but many associations have rules pertaining to the placement of commercial vehicles.

- Pets can be a big issue. Some associations will allow pets, but only pets of a certain type or size. You may not be able to have pets at all, even though you are an owner of your living space.
- It's insane to think that you could buy a co-op and not be allowed to have children living in it, right? Well, it may sound crazy, but it is possible that children will not be allowed in a development.
- Do you work from home? Better check the bylaws of any unit you're considering buying, because you may not be allowed to operate a home-based business from your unit.
- Thinking of washing your car this weekend? You may not be allowed to wash your car in the parking area near your condo or co-op. Check it out.

Recreational Vehicles

Recreational vehicles are often prohibited from general parking areas in planned communities. Many associations provide a separate parking area for boats, travel trailers, motor homes, and other RVs. It's not uncommon for the RV parking area to be surrounded by a sturdy fence. But, if you think that you can park your pop-up camper in your spare parking spot in the main parking lot, you could be in for a surprise. This type of restriction is not limited to condos and co-ops. It can apply to detached homes that are located within an association-run subdivision.

On the surface, having a special parking area for RVs doesn't sound so bad. But, did the salesperson tell you that there is a waiting list for space in the lot? Probably not. If you are getting the sales hype, you hear about the existence of a parking lot reserved for RVs. You don't necessarily learn of the waiting list until after you have entered into a purchase agreement.

Do you want your bass boat or motor home in a parking lot that you can't keep an eye on? Even with a fence and a security system, you may feel that your prized possession is at risk. Worse yet, suppose you can't get a spot in the lot. What will you do with your RV? This is a very real concern in some communities. If you own, or plan to own, an RV, check into this type of restrictive condition long before you make a purchase commitment.

Commercial Vehicles

Commercial vehicles are often prohibited from parking in community parking lots. If you own your own business or drive a company vehicle, this could be a heavy detriment to you. Let's assume that you are a plumber. The company you work for provides you with a truck for business and personal use. This truck is lettered with the company name and phone number. It has a pipe rack on it and a utility body. There is no question that the vehicle looks like what it is: a commercial vehicle. If this is your only source of transportation, what are you going to do when you receive notice that the truck cannot be parked in the community parking lot?

Many homeowner associations for condos, co-ops, and detached housing communities have a prohibition against commercial vehicles being garaged at the property address. A plumber can come fix your leaking faucet and park in your driveway or parking spot, but you can't keep a commercial vehicle in the spot on a regular basis. Is this fair? I don't think so. The concept is understandable, but the restriction is a hardship on business owners and employees who drive company vehicles.

Why would an association invoke such a rule? The reason is simple. Associations want the exterior conditions of their communities to be clean and inviting. A fleet of commercial vehicles could ruin the image of the community. Whether you drive a tractor-trailer truck, a plumbing truck, or a company car, you could be denied parking privileges. This type of rule is meant to protect the community, but it could deal you a dastardly blow. Check it out.

Pets

Pets are often a volatile issue. Should you be allowed to have pets in a home that you are paying for? I would say so, but many associations don't agree with me. Is it fair to allow cats, but to prohibit dogs? I don't think so, but a lot of associations do. Does a no-pet policy mean that you can have a pet parakeet or an aquarium full of fish? It may mean this exactly. If you are a pet person, you'd better check all restrictions very carefully to assure that you can have what you want. For example, you may be allowed to have a dog, as long as the animal doesn't exceed a certain weight. Don't think that just because you see residents walking their little lap dogs that you can bring your big dog into the complex.

Children

The issue of children in condos and co-ops is a hot issue. There are developments where children are not welcome. California, to the best of my knowledge, has ruled that children cannot be excluded as residents, and other states are looking at the issue. Is the prohibition of children an act of discrimination? It all depends on who you ask. Some condo and co-op associations pitch their developments as being adult-only complexes or retirement communities. In states where the prohibition of children within a complex is legal, you can face a difficult situation.

Reports show that most condo buyers are first-time home buyers. This would tend to indicate that the buyers are young. Couples who are young often start a family within a few years. How would you feel about buying a condo when you were first married and then being asked to leave once your first child was born? Chances are that you would be furious. But, it's possible that this could happen. If you have kids, or any inclination to have some, check the housing regulations very carefully.

My wife and I rented a nice house when we moved to Maine. The house was of a contemporary style and it fronted right on the water. We didn't have children when we rented it. Two years later, our daughter was born. We had always paid our rent on time and had taken very good care of the property. When our lease came up for renewal, we were forced to leave, since we had an infant in our family. This was legal, but hardly fair. In our case, the house was just a rental, but if I had purchased the property and been forced to relocate, I can't imagine the anger I would have felt. Don't laugh off restrictions as some mumbo jumbo on paper that don't mean anything. The terms and conditions to which you agree in the purchase of real estate are not generally flexible, so rely only on the written word.

Business Operations

Many condos and co-ops have some form of prohibition against conducting business operations from a dwelling unit. This may have no effect, whatsoever, on you. On the other hand, it can be a major problem. More and more people are working from home. It's a cost-effective approach to self-employment in our modern times. With modems, fax machines, email, and all of the other remote services that can be set up in a home office, working from home has never been more appealing. Yet, you may not be allowed to conduct business from your home if you buy a condo or co-op.

What, is the co-op police going to come raid my apartment and confiscate my computer? No, there are some types of home businesses that can be run profitably without any external evidence that business is being conducted. But, if your business requires people to come to your home, you could have a problem. If other residents of your community complain about heavy traffic in the parking lot and around your dwelling, you could become the focus of attention. Being prohibited from doing business out of your unit, of course, could be a major problem.

If you are conducting business in your unit without the complexity of customers or sales representatives calling upon you, it is very unlikely that anyone will complain. But, if your business is creating parking problems for other residents or a lot of foot traffic, someone may blow the whistle on you. Any ideas you might have for putting up a sign or other visible indication of running a business will almost certainly draw some fire from your association. Tread lightly if you plan to run a business out of your condo or co-op.

Washing Your Car

Surely, you're allowed to wash your car, right? Not necessarily. Many projects prohibit the washing or repair of automobiles on community property. What, I can't even wash my car in front of my own condo? Maybe not? It is not at all uncommon for planned communities to have prohibitions against shade-tree mechanics and car washing. Again, this may not seem fair, but it can reflect the reality of a situation. Some communities simply don't see this type of activity as being acceptable.

You might think I'm making this stuff up. Well, I'm not. As a real estate broker, builder, and developer, I've run the gamut of residential restrictions. Some of them are absurd. Others are sensible. You have to make the final call in your own interest. All I'm doing is making you aware of some, but not all, of the potential restrictions that you may encounter. Personally, I would not be happy living in a community where I was told what I could and could not do on simple issues. This is not a problem for some people. It is not my intent to turn you against condos or co-ops. I only want you to have enough facts to make your own informed decision. And, I can tell you that there are homeowner associations that prohibit car care in public view. If you want to do the work in your personal, enclosed garage—fine, but don't do it out in the open. There are some complexes that are not so strict. Don't stereotype the system. Consult the rules, regulations, and restrictions (before you buy) to determine if there are elements that will cause you grief.

Window Coverings

Most homes have some type of window coverings. They may be blinds, drapes, or pull-down shades. Are you aware that your complex may stipulate the type of window coverings that you may employ? Don't laugh, it's true. I've seen restrictions that required window coverings and not only coverings, but coverings of particular types. Are you willing to let an association tell you what type of curtains you must hang in your windows? It's all in the best interest of the community—at least that's what you are likely to be told. I know that I'm pulling out some petty stuff here, but it is representative of what you might run into. Don't take anything for granted. Check out restrictions thoroughly before you buy into a development. Very simple elements may play a part in making you uncomfortable.

CHANGING THE RULES

If you buy a condo or co-op, you will have to live by the decisions of your board of directors. There will be means of change available to you, but accomplishing any significant change can be like climbing a gravel mountain. For every step you take towards the top, you are likely to slide back several steps. It is never easy to change the minds of the masses.

Buying into a development is a big decision. You are a part of the condo community, but not the whole condo community unto yourself. If you don't like being a single cog in the mechanism, condo and co-op life probably is not right for you. Most importantly, you have to be comfortable with the rules you must live by. Don't assume that you can make sweeping changes in the government or regulation of your community. If you are not comfortable with existing rules and regulations, you should find a different community in which to live.

I can't stress enough the importance of having competent legal council review all documents pertaining to your purchase before a final commitment is made. What may read like a rock-solid agreement to you could be full of legal loopholes. Find a seasoned professional to help you, and rely on that person's wisdom. If you want to be extra safe, retain a second advisor to commit on the decision of your first advisor.

It has been said that the purchase of a home is usually the single most important step in the financial life of an adult. This is often true. If you buy into a development in which you are not happy, it could take years and a lot of lost money to get out of your situation. This can be avoided if you spend enough time researching your decision before making a decision to buy. It's your life, your home, and your decision—make it wisely.

CHAPTER 6

Condos Versus Co-ops: Pros and Cons

If you are trying to decide between buying a condo or a co-op, you have a confusing situation on your hands. At first glance, there doesn't seem to be much difference between the two types of living spaces. You know there must be differences, but you can't put your finger on them. As a wise buyer, you want to review all of your options carefully, before making a buying decision.

The difference between condos and co-ops ranges from location to administration. There are many factors to consider. Even after you narrow your decision to one type of living space, you still have a lot of sorting out to do. Many of the advantages that you will seek may be of a personal nature. Some of what you need to know, however, is on a different level. The previous chapters have given you a glimpse of differences between condos and co-ops, but this chapter digs in and gives you a much stronger comparison.

DO YOU WANT TO OWN PAPER OR AIR?

Do you want to own paper or air? This may be one of the first questions you have to ask yourself when considering condos and co-ops as housing options. What do you really own when you buy into a co-op? The answer is *paper*, the stock issued to you by the co-op corporation. A condo purchase results in a recorded deed, but the deed is for air space only. Neither of these types of purchases are the same as a traditional real estate purchase. Condos come closer to being a traditional purchase, but they still don't offer full ownership of the real estate.

Some people will say that you would be foolish to buy a place to live where you would have only paper or air to show for your purchase. You may even be one of them. If you are, divert your attention away from condos and co-ops right now. However, a lot of people feel co-ops and condos are the way of the future. It makes sense when you consider the high cost of land and the shrinking environment (due to wildlife refuges, wetlands, shopping centers, office complexes, ski slopes, and housing developments) we have for housing.

So, do you still want to consider buying a condo or a co-op? If you're reading this book, you probably do. Ask yourself a few questions. Can you accept the fact that you will not own the ground on which your home is situated? Are you willing to pay regular association dues to cover your portion of operating expenses, maintenance costs, and related expenses? Can you live comfortably in close proximity of others? If you are giving affirmative answers to these questions, you show potential as a condo or co-op buyer.

ISSUES TO CONSIDER WHEN CHOOSING BETWEEN A CONDO AND CO-OP

Once you get past the point of being concerned about owning only paper or air, you are ready to move onto more comparisons. You already know that condos and co-ops share many similarities. Now, it is time to see how they differ and how the differences may affect you.

PETS

Pets are often an issue for people to consider. Some people love animals. Others can live without them. Even among pet lovers,

CONDO OR CO-OP?

Will you be better off with a condo or a co-op? It depends on your needs and desires. Let's look at a comparison of the two. In the following table, a column with an "X" in it denotes the living arrangement with the most benefits. An "X" in both columns indicates that both types of dwelling units are accommodating.

TOPIC	Condo	Co-Op
Pets	X	
Parking	X	X
Unit Size	X	
Storage	X	
Utility Costs	X	X
Services Provided	X	X
Restrictions	X	X
Paying off Mortgage	X	
Selling Your Unit	X	
Tax Advantages	X	
Resale Value	X	
Acquisition Cost		X
Corporate Failure	X	
Privacy	X	
Safety	X	

there is often a difference of opinion regarding which pets are best. For example, a dog lover may not care for cats. Are you a pet person? Do you want to keep pets in your new home? If so, check the rules and regulations of each development you are considering. Many condos allow owners to keep pets on the premises. Some co-ops allow pets. There may be, however, restrictions pertaining to the size and type of pet that can be kept. You may even find developments that have a no-pets policy. Based on my experience, I feel that your odds of having the pet of your choice are better in a condo than in a co-op. But, this may not always be the case.

Co-ops are almost always converted apartment buildings. This typically means that the living space is small and the exterior grounds are limited. Neither of these conditions is conducive to the comfort of large pets. Condos, on the other hand, can be quite large, and they can be situated on several acres of open ground. This tends to be a better environment for large pets. Don't assume that co-ops are out just because you want a pet, but I think you will find condos more suitable in this regard.

PARKING

Parking can be a problem in some developments. Many developments that are the result of apartment conversions have limited parking facilities. In big cities, where privately-owned cars are not the most common form of transportation, this is not such a problem. However, in many cities, people own and drive their own vehicles. It is common for a typical household to have at least two vehicles, and sometimes more. Finding a development that will allocate more than two parking spaces to a single dwelling unit can be a challenge.

Co-ops may offer less parking than condo developments. The reason is simple. Co-ops are generally found in major cities, where privately-owned cars are not used as much as buses, taxis, and subways. Since co-ops are typically the result of an apartment conversion, the existing parking lot is all that is available. Condo developments that are built, rather than converted, can design adequate parking into the development plans. For a person who owns more than one vehicle, a condo might be a better choice.

Unit Size

Condos usually offer a greater range of sizes to choose from than co-ops. Since most co-ops were rental apartments before being converted, they are limited in size. Condos can fall into the same situation. Plenty of condos are the result of apartment conversions. I don't want you to think that all condos are brand new and spacious. However, it is easier to find condos that are newer and larger than it is to locate co-ops with similar qualities. For example, getting two bathrooms in a co-op can be extremely difficult. New condos, however, can have two or more bathrooms without any problem. The cost to buy such a unit will be higher, but at least you will be getting the features that you desire.

Storage

Storage is often a problem for homeowners of all types. There never seems to be enough space to store everything you own. The storage issue is a serious one in both co-ops and condos. Will your co-op building provide you with basement storage that is secure? Can you have an outside storage building next to your condo? What will the overall storage capacity be? For that matter, how many closets will your unit have, and how large will they be?

Some condos are sold with attached garages. This is one place you can consider for use as storage, but the garages are not usually large. If you want to park your car in the garage, there may not be a lot of room left over for storage. Will your unit have attic space that can be used for storage? It's likely that a condo might, but it would be rare to find a co-op with attic storage. Maybe your condo will be built on a full foundation that allows private basement storage. If you have basement storage in a co-op, it will be shared space of some sort. Security might leave a lot to be desired in a co-op storage facility. This can also be the case with condos that are clustered together on a common foundation.

Condos tend to have the upper hand when it comes to storage space. For one thing, many condos are larger than most co-ops. And, the design features in new condos are often centered around a modern lifestyle. Old buildings that are converted may not have enough storage space to handle modern life.

INSIDER TIP

If you are buying into an older development, make sure that you will have proper and adequate storage for your personal possessions. Many old buildings offer extremely limited storage for unit owners. Quality developments will often provide outside storage sheds for unit storage, and fenced, secure areas for boats, RVs, and so forth. Older buildings may offer nothing more than a chicken-wire enclosure in the basement.

Utility Costs

The cost of utilities depends on many factors. What type of heating and cooling systems are being used? How well insulated is the building? This type of questioning must come into play before you can compare two units equally. There are, however, some design factors to take into consideration when comparing condos to co-ops in terms of utility costs.

Let's say that you are looking at a two-bedroom co-op on the second floor of a building. The co-op unit is located near the middle of the building. This means that there is only one outside wall in the unit. The front wall meets a hall. Both side walls have other co-ops opposite of them. Being on the second floor, your unit will gain some heat from the unit below it. The units beside yours will shelter it from cold conditions. This type of unit should be less expensive to heat than one that is located on the corner of the building. A corner unit will have two outside walls that could let in the cold.

Assume that a co-op conversion is being done. To enable each resident to have a separate utility bill, electric, baseboard heat is installed in each co-op unit. This is about the least expensive route for the developer to take. Putting an individual heat pump in each unit would cost much more, and space may be a problem for such an installation. So, the converted co-op winds up with electric heat.

Another factor of the co-op conversion is the insulation in the walls. Windows and doors are also a consideration. If the windows and doors are old, they are not likely to come close to the energy-efficient levels of modern building materials. Insulation may or may not be added to the exterior walls and attics of a co-op building. All of this comes into play when calculating heating and cooling expenses.

A condo that is the result of a conversion could wind up with similar qualities of a co-op. However, if a condo development is being built from the ground up, modern materials will be used. Building codes require minimum standards. It's very likely that an efficient heating and cooling system will be used.

The acquisition cost of the condo will be greater, but the long-range savings may offset the cost. Again, condos seem to have an advantage over co-ops.

Services Provided

Is there much difference in the services that condos and co-ops provide to residents? Some of the standard services condos and co-ops typically offer are pest control, building repairs, grounds maintenance, snow removal, possibly on-site security, and so forth. There will, naturally, be great differences from one development to another. You will have to check each association to see what they have to offer you.

The quality of service you receive as a resident is dependent upon the people in power. If you have a strong association and a solid board of directors, you should get the services promised to you. In terms of comparing condos to co-ops in this arena, I'd say it's a tied ball game.

Nonpayment of Dues

If you don't pay your association dues, co-op developments probably have more control over you than do condo developments. It's very likely that the co-op corporation can evict you for the non-payment of dues. You may be ejected from your home and forced to watch the living space you paid for be rented to another tenant. The co-op corporation may even be able to sell your unit to a willing buyer, whether you authorize the sale or not. This is serious business.

In the case of a condo, your association can't evict you. The board of directors may decide to put a lien on your property for the unpaid dues, but you will have your day in court. And, your condo won't be rented out to someone else or sold out from under you. This, in my mind, is a big advantage over a

DANGER ALERT!

If you fail to pay your association dues as a co-op owner, you can be evicted from your dwelling unit and your unit may be sold to someone else. This does not happen when you own a condo.

co-op. Few people ever plan to not pay their bills. But, when unexpected hardships occur, the ability to meet financial obligations may be hindered. Personally, I consider a resident who cannot pay his or her dues to be much safer in a condo than in a co-op.

The scenario previously presented may not always hold true. You and your attorney will have to investigate each development carefully for their methods of dealing with non-payment of dues. Not all co-ops will put you out in the street, but never assume that your eviction is not a possibility.

Paying Off the Mortgage

Paying off the mortgage on a condo is very similar to paying it off in any other type of home ownership. The mortgage loan is in your name. Each month, you make mortgage payments for the principal and interest. When the mortgage is paid off, you own your condo. It's as simple as that.

This is not the case with a co-op. When you buy into a co-op, you don't have a personal mortgage on the building or unit. The co-op corporation holds the mortgage loan, and you pay a portion of the mortgage payment in your association dues. What do you have when the mortgage is paid off? You have a lease for your co-op unit and stock that is more valuable. You still don't own any real property. This is not especially bad, but it is something that you should be aware of.

Selling Your Unit

Selling a co-op unit can be much more difficult than selling a condo unit. This is because most co-op boards have more control and power than average condo boards have. This is due, at least in part, to the fact that co-op owners are only stockholders. Condo owners have a deed to their air space. Co-op owners have only a lease. The different structure of the two types of organizations is what makes it possible for the co-op board to be stronger.

DANGER ALERT!

Selling your interest in a co-op can be much more difficult than selling a condo. Most co-op boards have control over the sale of stock in a co-op development. You may find that you are restricted in many ways when you decide to sell or lease your interest in a co-op.

A condo association cannot dictate to whom you sell your unit. Co-op associations can control who you sell your shares of stock to. This is a huge issue to consider, and it is definitely a strike against co-ops. I sure wouldn't want a corporate structure sitting over me and presiding over potential buyers for my unit until one that was suitable was found. This simply doesn't seem fair to a seller, but it is the reality of many co-op sale situations.

Not only can a co-op board hold a heavy hand in the decision of to whom you sell, the board can prohibit you from leasing your unit to some other person. Remember, you are a lessee in a co-op arrangement, so subletting could be prohibited. This would not be the case in a condo, because you own the rights to the property. Again, we have a severe strike against co-ops. Is there a pattern developing here? Are condos the best way to go?

A lot of people think so, but you may find reasons to pursue a co-op.

Tax Advantages

If you are interested in tax advantages—and who isn't?—condos will likely provide you with greater savings. When you buy a condo, you have your own home mortgage. You pay all of the principal and interest on your loan. Additionally, you pay all of the property taxes for your unit. A portion of these expenses should be tax deductible. Check with your accountant to determine your precise tax advantages.

Buying into a co-op should provide you with some tax deductions, but they are unlikely to be as great as what you would gain with a condo purchase. In a co-op, you are paying a portion of the loan expenses and taxes. You can probably deduct some of this expense from your personal income taxes. Again, check with your tax advisor to see exactly what your circumstances will allow.

Resale Value

How do condos and co-ops stack up in terms of resale value? This is a difficult question to answer. There is not a clear-cut answer to the question. Condos in one development may not hold their value, while co-ops in another part of the city may rapidly escalate in value. Or, the roles could be reversed. Real estate values can be fickle. Condos usually hold their values well. This is also true of good co-op developments. If I had to venture a guess as to which type of residence would show the strongest equity gain, I would bet on the condo. But, every situation has the potential to perform in its own way. Even if you compile a huge stack of statistics, you can't be sure how a particular property will do.

Acquisition Cost

Is there much difference in the price of a condo compared to that of a co-op? It's difficult to say which type of living space will be more expensive. Location, unit size, and amenities all affect the price. Some condos are very similar to co-ops in their size and design. It's not unusual for the only notable difference to be in the type of ownership a person has. Under these conditions, it could be a toss up on price. However, the condo would probably be more expensive, due to the nature of the ownership.

Many condos are not created from converted apartments. New condos are almost always more expensive than co-op units. But again, location and amenities have much to do with a property value. You must look into local prices and find out for yourself, firsthand, which units cost more and why they do.

Corporate Failure

The corporate failure of a co-op corporation can lead to bankruptcy. Owning stock in a bankrupt corporation doesn't leave you with a lot to show for your purchase of a co-op. Condo associations can fail, but you will still have your deed to the air space in your condo. When a development fails, it's bad for all the residents. Condo owners are in a stronger position than co-op owners during such a failure. Residents suffer in either type of development if a financial crisis occurs, so check out the financial stability of all developments before you buy into one.

DANGER ALERT

Co-op developments are owned by corporations, and corporations can file for bankruptcy. Check the financial strength of any co-op into which you are considering buying.

Privacy

You often relinquish your privacy when you choose to live in mass housing. If you live under the same roof as all the other residents of your community, you are bound to give up some privacy. Co-ops are generally structured so that you live in the equivalent of an apartment. Some developments are built better than others, but none of them afford residents a lot of privacy. Condos, however, can be built in a manner that will give you much greater privacy. You will have to assess each individual property to see if it meets your minimum criteria.

INSIDER TIP

Condo developers can incorporate tactics to improve privacy for residents. A common practice is to erect privacy fencing around a lawn, deck, or patio. Selected landscaping can add to privacy. Even window placement and the types of windows used can affect privacy. Shop around. Look at many developments before making a buying decision.

Safety

What, if any, steps have been taken towards safety in the development that you are considering? Keep in mind there are different forms of safety. Fire safety, for instance, is always a serious issue in mass housing. Co-ops are generally converted from old buildings. The extent of the conversion has a lot to do with the quality of the building. If an old apartment building is turned into a co-op without modernization, the safety factors will be lower than if the building undergoes a complete make-over. Has the electrical wiring been upgraded? Are the walls fire-resistant? Does the building meet or exceed all local building codes?

Old buildings will often pass code inspections only because they are existing buildings. If a new building was being built to the exact specifications of an existing building, the new building might never pass code inspections. When a conversion project is done, the property might be required to be brought up to current code requirements. This makes the project more expensive, but it should make it safer for residents. When new buildings are built, they must comply with local codes. Knowing this, buying a new condo might make more sense than buying a converted condo or co-op. You have to weigh all of the factors for yourself.

MORE SAFETY CONSIDERATIONS

Condos and co-ops vary in safety precautions. Does the development have limited auto access? Are security people on the premises? Do residents have special door keys or cards for alcove doors? If you are looking at condos, can you get one with an attached garage that will reduce contact with waiting criminals? Condos have the potential advantage of (in many cases) offering private garages, but they can be more remote and not as well lighted as a co-op building. Safety issues are a matter of personal preference. The key is to investigate what you will be getting if you buy into a development.

What's the bottom line when comparing condos to co-ops? Ultimately, the decision of which type of housing arrangement is best must be made by the buyer. Personally, I prefer condos over co-ops. My feelings are shared by many people, but not by all. Co-ops have their place in life, and a co-op might be the ideal way of life for you. What it all boils down to is that you have to decide which type of home in which you will be more comfortable.

CHAPTER 7

Buying New or Used, You Need the Right People to Work With

How will you look for the home of your dreams? Are you going to read classified ads in the newspaper? Will you look for large display ads that promote a certain development? Do you need the assistance of a buyer's broker? Do you know what a buyer's broker is? These questions are only the beginning of what you have to consider when you start your search for the perfect home.

When buying a condo or a co-op, you may be working with brokers, developers, or private owners. In fact, it's very possible that you will be working with at least two out of three in this group. There is no rule that says you must work with a broker, but many buyers do. There are both pros and cons to working with real estate professionals. If you deal directly with a developer, you might get a super deal. Or, you might get taken to the cleaners, so to speak. Buying from a private owner can produce a good deal, but it can also be risky. The more you know about working with the various people involved in your home purchase, the less likely you are to have a bad experience.

LOOKING FOR YOUR HOME: HOW TO GET STARTED

There are a number of ways to look for a condo or co-op. You may see billboards or other advertisements that bring your attention to a particular community of condos or a co-op building. A lot of people like to get out and roam from development to development, looking at model homes. This is a good way to get to know what is available to you. For-sale ads in your local newspaper is another way to find out what the market has to offer. Calling a real estate brokerage is one of the fastest ways to see what's available in your area. All of these methods can be effective, so what will you do?

Shopping for a new home without the help of a real estate broker can save you some money. It can also cost you more than you would ever hope to save. The right real estate broker is an asset, not a liability. However, finding the right broker can take some time. If you get hooked up with the wrong brokers, your buying experience can be worse than if you go it alone.

Buying directly from a seller who is not represented by a brokerage should be a cheaper way to go. It often is. But, you may not be protected as well with disclosure forms and representations when you deal directly with a seller. Most, if not all states require licensed realty professionals to follow certain rules that are intended to protect both buyers and sellers. Most home buyers should find a reliable buyer's broker to work with in the seeking and purchasing of a home.

Real Estate Brokerages

Are you interested in working with a real estate brokerage? If you are, the brokerage is a good place to begin your search. Most brokerages are tied into some form of multiple-listing service. This gives agents and brokers access to homes that are listed for sale by any brokerage within the multiple-listing organization. There are some risks and drawbacks to dealing with a brokerage, as are discussed later in this chapter. If you are the type of person who doesn't want to work with a brokerage, you are going to have to do most of your searching on your own. This can be time consuming, but effective, and of course less expensive.

There is nothing wrong with going through model homes and checking out ads in the local newspaper. However, working with a brokerage is normally the easiest, and often the least frustrating, way of finding a home that meets your needs. A broker can help you in many ways, but you must make sure that you understand the role of the broker completely. If you decide to work by yourself, it is a good idea to meet with your banker and your lawyer before you start looking for a new home.

Professionals You Should Consult

The process of buying a home can be a complicated one. It can also take a long time. To cut down on the processing time and the confusion, you should consider consulting with both your attorney and your lender early in the process. In doing so, you can put the wheels of the process in motion. Many lenders will begin a pre-purchase financing approval upon request. A good lawyer can advise you on questions to ask and answers to seek. The sooner you get to the professionals, the sooner you are likely to expedite the entire process.

Your Banker

Your banker can sit down with you and go over your financial standing. By doing this, the lender can determine how much money you will be allowed to borrow for the purchase of a home. This is a great first step to take. There is no sense in looking at properties that are out of your financial reach. Your banker will be able to tell you about different types of loan programs, and there are many to choose from. You will find out how much money you will need for a down payment. Closing costs and points are other expenses that your banker can help you to understand and anticipate. In many cases, it's possible to make a loan application and become pre-approved for a home loan, based on a hypothetical situation. If you do this, you will know that money is waiting for you when you find the perfect home. Visiting your banker before you invest a lot of time in your search for a place to live is always a good idea.

Your Lawyer

Your lawyer is someone else you should consult before getting too far along in your housing hunt. Lawyers can explain expenses, such as closing costs, so that you will understand and anticipate them. The lawyer you choose should be someone who has extensive experience in real estate matters. Not all lawyers do, and you deserve representation by someone who is an expert in the field of real estate. In addition to explaining terms and expenses, your lawyer can give you tips on what to look for and what to look out for. You should never sign any type of real estate agreement without first having your attorney review it.

Most people don't talk to a lawyer until they are well into their home purchase. This can be a mistake. The sooner you seek legal help, the less likely you are to make a costly mistake. There are many legal aspects to a real estate purchase, and you should have someone to guide you through them. Establish a relationship with an attorney early on. By doing this, you will gain knowledge and the advantage of having someone you know that you can call on when questions come up.

APPROACHES TO BUYING YOUR HOME

There are basically four different approaches to take when buying a condo or a co-op. You can buy into a development that is in full existence. This is generally a safe way to buy, but it can also be the most expensive way. If you prefer, you can buy a unit before it's built. Doing this will almost guarantee you the lowest price, but the risk is greater. The final approach is to buy a unit that has been lived in previously. Of all the ways to buy a condo or a co-op, buying one that has been lived in should be the safest way of all.

FOUR WAYS TO BUY YOUR HOME

- Buy a new condo or co-op that is already built.
- Buy a used condo or co-op from the previous owner.
- Buy a condo or co-op that is under construction or conversion.
- Buy a unit before it is built or converted.

Why is buying a used unit safer? If you are buying an existing unit in a building that has been operating for some time, you can check the track record of the development. Have association dues gone up much over the years? Are the residents in the building happy? What are the average utility costs? All of these questions, and many more, can be answered when you buy a used condo or co-op. This type of information will not be available for units that have never held residents.

Am I saying that you should only buy a unit if it has been lived in and has a track record? No, absolutely not. There are downsides to buying used units. For example, warranties that you would get with a new unit may not exist on a used unit. Older buildings are likely to need costly maintenance and repair sooner than new buildings. There are always trade-offs to consider.

Once you make up your mind which phase of a condo or co-op in which you are interested in buying, you can narrow the parameters of your search. For example, if you know you want to buy a unit in an established, proven building, you have no reason to waste time looking at brand-new units. On the other hand, if you have decided to buy a unit that is being sold by plans (one that doesn't exist yet), you can rule out existing units and concentrate your efforts on developers. The more you can narrow the field, the easier it will be for you to avoid confusion.

DEVELOPERS

Developers are the people who decide to make condos and co-ops available. Without developers and builders, there would not be condos or co-ops. Someone with a vision has to take the initiative to create housing. Some projects soar and others sink. A developer who has a successful track record is likely to maintain the success, but there is no guarantee of it. You can tell which developers are good ones and which ones are not so good if you know what to look for.

INSIDER TIP

Buying directly from the developer of a housing project can result in a much lower price. However, there are some additional risks associated with doing a direct-buy.

If you want to buy a condo or a co-op, there is a strong possibility that you will deal with a developer at some point in your home acquisition. Dealing directly with a developer can result in a lower purchase price. If a developer is not paying a commission to a real estate brokerage, a unit can be sold for less, and the developer still maintains the same profit level. But dealing directly with a seller, without a mediator in the middle, can increase the risks of buying real estate. If you don't know what questions to ask or what to look for, you could buy into trouble without realizing it until it's too late. Your attorney can help you avoid this.

When developers build or convert a housing project, they often list the dwelling units with a real estate brokerage. Some developers have their own staff of in-house sales professionals. Most developers are willing to work with real estate agents and brokers, even if the property is not listed with a brokerage. Some small developers act as their own salesperson. Typically, however, your first encounters as a prospective buyer will be with either a brokerage representative or an in-house sales staff. It's unlikely that you will talk face-to-face with the developer.

When you consider a new development, about what should you be the most concerned? Consider first whether the developer is reputable. Find out if the developer has a successful track record. Don't rule any developer out, but it helps to build a comfort level if you can see past success from the same developer from whom you may buy.

It is risky to buy a condo or a co-op that is proposed or under construction. However, buying directly from a developer, before units are completed, can result in significant savings. We will go into more detail on this subject later in this chapter. For now, let's concentrate on developers. There is no reason why you shouldn't deal with developers. As with any deal, you have to pay attention to what you are doing, but most developers will treat you as fairly as any other seller.

Some people fear developers. There have been people who have told me that they were sure developers would take advantage of them. It's possible that a developer will take advantage of buyers, but any seller could also attempt to do this. Regardless of with whom you are dealing, you have to be

DANGER ALERT!

Buying a condo or a co-op that is not yet built or converted can produce almost instant equity and a low purchase price, but you may not get what you think you are going to get. There is always risk associated with reward, so act carefully.

careful. If you have a good attorney and run all aspects of your activity past the lawyer, you should be safe.

The biggest risks associated with buying from developers is not related directly to the developers. Your risk is in what you are buying, not from whom you are buying it. Since developers are typically selling new buildings or units that have been recently converted, there is less historical information on which to base a buying decision. This is where the real risk is. Some people fear developers, but I feel this fear is unfounded.

Private Owners

Is it not necessarily safer to buy a home from a private owner who is looking to sell. The safe part is that you may be able to research the building, the unit, and the association to see what past performances have proved. This is an advantage. But, private sellers may not be as forthcoming with information as a developer might be. Does this surprise you? Developers often go to extreme lengths to avoid legal problems. Some private sellers are either ignorant of disclosure laws or choose to ignore them. I'm not saying that a private seller is likely to swindle you, but a person could be uninformed of what types of disclosures are typically required in the sale of a home.

Many people think that you can get your best deal when you buy from a private seller. In some cases, you can. If the person is involved in a divorce or is having financial difficulties, you might be able to acquire property from the individual at a very low price. It is not unusual, however, for private sellers to demand more money for their real estate than a developer would. Why? The individual is selling a home, the home that the individual has lived in and become attached to. Sentimental value has its place, but the place is not in the price tag of a home. Developers are generally realistic. They normally price their properties at, or below market rates. Many private sellers don't do this.

Have you ever gone into a discount store to buy an item that was advertised at a low sale price? If so, how often have you bought other items while you were in the store? You might have assumed that all the products in the store were sold at discounted prices, and then found it for a much lower price in another store. Well, perceptions can deceive you. Don't fall into the trap of assuming that private sellers will give you the best deal. It's entirely possible that a private seller will give you a good price, but make sure you confirm just how good the price actually is before you make a buying decision.

Some people claim that developers are slick business sharks. I don't doubt that some are, but it's unlikely that you will find a majority of developers to be shysters and sharks. Are all private sellers honest? Not likely. It's like buying the used car from the little, old lady from Pasadena, who only drove it to church on Sundays. There are good and bad deals in the marketplace. Likewise, there are honest and dishonest sellers in the arena. The players don't wear hats or uniforms that distinguish the good from the bad. You have to sort out each deal on an individual basis.

Private sellers are rarely in positions to help you with financing. Many developers have established relationships with lenders and can assist you in your financing. It's sort of like buying a car from a dealer rather than from a private owner. The dealer usually has a variety of loan packages from which you can choose. It can be much the same way when you deal with a developer. Private sellers don't have the opportunity to help you in the same way.

Will a private seller help you with the expense of your closing costs? It's very likely that you can arrange this. Developers often build some additional money into the price of a unit to help buyers with their financing expenses. If a private seller is willing, you can structure a similar deal. Is a private seller going to pay for your moving expenses? Probably not, but a developer might. Many developers are willing to get creative in their pricing, financing, and terms. Some private sellers will do this, too, but many of them are not familiar enough with the procedure to do it well.

So, what am I saying about buying from a private owner? There are pros and cons. You gain the advantage of a unit with a track record. But, the unit has been lived in. Buying from a private seller might save you money, but it might not. Few private sellers will give you incentives for buying their home. A lot of developers will offer incentives to purchasers. What's the bottom line? There is no iron-clad answer. Find the home you want, and then work out a deal with whoever is selling it. Make sure, however, to run all aspects of the process by your attorney.

REAL ESTATE BROKERAGES

A large majority of home buyers work with real estate brokerages when searching for and buying a home. Brokerages can be very helpful and beneficial to prospective home buyers. Rarely is there any real detriment to working with a brokerage. Some people feel that they can save money if they don't work with a brokerage. It's true that most brokerages are paid a commission when a sale is made, but there is no guarantee that a seller would accept a lower price, even if a brokerage was not involved. The right brokerage and brokerage representative can be extremely beneficial to you. Conversely, the wrong assistance can be a nightmare.

Big or Small

Does it make much difference if the brokerage I choose is big or small? As a buyer, it shouldn't make much difference to you how large the brokerage with whom you choose to work is. The individual agent or broker who represents you is what you must concentrate on. Yes, it's nice to have a long-standing, reputable brokerage in your home court, but it is the individual broker who will decide the outcome of your buying experience. There are advantages to using large companies when you wish to sell your home, but I can't think of any real advantage to it when buying. However, make sure that your broker has full access to all multiple-listing services in the region.

Buyer's Brokers

The key to a successful relationship with a real estate broker is all in finding the right one. Just as some lawyers are not experts in real estate, some brokers and agents are not experts in condos and co-ops. If you are looking to buy a condo or co-op, you should find a professional who is familiar with this type of property. Furthermore, it will generally be best if you choose a buyer's broker. A buyer's broker is a broker who works for you, the buyer, but who can be paid by anyone, including a seller. Traditional brokers work for sellers and with buyers. Buyer's brokers work for buyers. There is a big difference, and the results of your happiness may depend on it. Let me explain.

INSIDER TIP

When you choose to work with a real estate professional during the purchase of your new home, make sure that you acquire the services of a Buyer's Broker.

Why Do You Want a Buyer's Broker?

When I explain the role of traditional brokers to my clients, I often use lawyers to illustrate my point. Assume, for the moment, that you were about to become involved in a fierce legal battle with your neighbor. The dispute could be about anything. You find out that your neighbor has retained an attorney to represent the case against you. Now it's your turn to get a lawyer. Would you hire the same one that your neighbor did? Not likely. It probably would not be in your best interest for you and your foe to share the same representation. This makes sense, doesn't it? Okay, now let's put it in terms of real estate.

You are about to buy a condo. A decision has been made to work with a real estate brokerage. You go into a brokerage and ask for assistance in buying a home. An agent shows you in-house listings of properties for sale, and you see a condo that interests you. The agent you are working with is working for the seller. Did you know this? Maybe, but do you understand the complications of the situation? It's doubtful. In a way, you are in a relationship similar to the one you would have been in, had you hired your neighbor's lawyer.

Traditional real estate agents and brokers have always worked for sellers, either directly or as sub-agents. Few buyers understand this. A broker may hand you a card or tell you that the seller is the client and that you are the customer. It might be stated clearly, in writing, that the broker is working for the seller. Still, a lot of buyers operate under an incorrect assumption that the broker is working for them. It is easy to get confused on this issue.

It's not uncommon for perspective home buyers to develop a relationship with the brokers with which they work. Brokers often take buyers out to lunch. This can build a certain bond. When a buyer asks for advice, the brokers they work with will often give it. You can see why a buyer, such as yourself, might think that the broker who is working with him is working for him. In reality, the broker is not.

Let's say that you've spent the last four weeks looking at co-ops with a broker. The broker has become your buddy. A co-op turns up that you really like. You decide to make an offer to purchase it. The price on the co-op is reasonable, but you want to make a lower offer, just to see what will happen. As the broker is helping you prepare your offer, you make a comment about how you are willing to pay full price, but you want to try a lower offer first. The broker smiles and continues filling out the purchase offer. Then, the broker goes to present your offer to the seller, who has her property listed with a different brokerage.

When "your" broker presents your offer to the seller's broker, she tells the other broker about the comment you made. Basically, the broker is letting the other broker know that you will come up on your price. The offer is presented to the seller, who counters it back at full price. You accept the deal and go on about life, never knowing that your confidence was breached. Did "your" broker do anything wrong? Absolutely not. She did exactly what is required of her. A seller's broker must treat buyers fairly, but the seller is always the one to whom a seller's broker must be loyal. In this example, the broker would have been wrong not to reveal your comment. Doesn't seem fair, does it? Maybe not, but you were working with a sub-agent of the seller, not a buyer's broker. See how the difference between brokers might affect you?

When you retain a buyer's broker, you have true representation from a person who has your best interest in mind. A buyer's broker not only works with you, but for you as well. However, don't assume that a buyer's broker can take the place of your attorney. Ideally, you should be represented by both an attorney and a buyer's broker.

Can I Afford a Buyer's Broker?

Won't hiring my own broker cost a lot more money? This is a question I've heard often. When you retain a buyer's broker, you enter into some form of agreement. How, when, and how much the broker will be paid is spelled out in the agreement. You can pay the broker out of your own funds, or you can ask the seller to pay the broker for you. Most sellers who are dealing with brokerages will not argue about having your broker paid out of an agreed-upon commission with the listing agency. In reality, it is the listing agency that pays your broker. The seller pays the listing agency, and that agency pays a split of the commission to your broker. The compensation is handled in about the same way that it always has been, but you derive more benefits, without paying extra for the privilege.

Bear in mind, not all sellers will pay your broker's fee, and you may run into a listing agency that will not agree to split up a commission. This is seldom the case, but it could happen.

WHO PAYS YOUR BUYER'S BROKER?

Anyone can pay a buyer's broker. The buyer is the client of the broker, but a seller can compensate the broker for services rendered. Deciding who is responsible for payment is done during the negotiation stage of a purchase, and it is not unusual for sellers to pay a buyer's broker.

Properties that are listed with multiple-listing services often show the percentage of compensation that will be paid from the listing agency to a buyer's broker. Talk to your attorney for precise advice on any agreement you enter into. This is the best way to protect yourself from unpleasant, and possibly costly, surprises.

Specialists

Let's talk about specialists in the real estate world. If you needed heart surgery, would you go to your family doctor to perform the operation? I doubt it; you would probably insist on a heart specialist. Am I right? Well then, shouldn't you consider hiring a specialist to help you find your condo or co-op? Since condos and co-ops are most abundant in heavily populated areas, it is generally easy to find buyer's brokers who specialize in various forms of real estate in these areas. Some concentrate solely on working with investors. Buyer's brokers may specialize in commercial property, detached homes in a certain price range, town houses, or any other form of real estate, including condos and co-ops.

How much do you really know about condos or co-ops? You are learning a lot with this book, but your knowledge probably can't compare with that of a seasoned specialist in the field. If you are going to retain a buyer's broker, you might as well get one who knows the ropes around condos and co-ops. How do you find such a broker? Look in your local phone directory. Advertisements in phone books frequently list specialties. Another approach is to call various brokers and ask in what they specialize. Don't tell them what type of property in which you are interested until after they tell you where their expertise lies. If you ask brokers if they specialize in condos, they might start doing so—with you as their first client. Hold your cards, and make them show you their hand first.

What is the benefit of using a specialist? Obviously, the more you do something, the better you should become at doing it. Brokers who concentrate on condos and co-ops should be up to date on what's hot and what's not. The brokers should know what's for sale, where the best deals are, and of what to warn you. A broker who sells mostly commercial property may have trouble understanding all of the paperwork associated with a condo or co-op association. This is not the case with a specialist who sells condos and co-ops regularly. It will be in your best interest to work with brokers who have a proven track record in the type of real estate you are interested in buying.

Don't Just Sign Up

Don't just sign up with the first buyer's broker with whom you talk. Interview several brokers. Make them work for your business. Get references from them. Find out what their track records are like. Are the fees for which they're asking in line with what you feel is fair to pay? How many condos or co-ops have the various brokers sold in the last year? Has the broker had special training in any particular field of real estate? Can you cancel your buyer's-broker agreement without penalty if you are dissatisfied with the broker's performance? Ask the brokers to give you five reasons why you should choose them over other brokers. This can produce some very interesting results. Brokers are not accustomed to being asked such a question, so these remarks should be from the heart, rather than out of a canned sales pitch. Just remember, the broker will be working for you, so make the professional earn your business.

WHICH TO BUY: NEW OR USED?

Where do you fit in as a condo or co-op buyer? Are you a gambler who is looking to make some fast money in an equity gain?

If so, deal directly with a developer and buy units that have not yet been built or converted. Do you feel more comfortable when someone helps you make tough decisions? A real estate broker can help you make decisions, as well as take a lot of your personal effort out of your quest. People who like a safety net under them may use a broker to help them buy an existing unit with a proven track record. Buying directly from a private owner who is selling a unit is somewhat of a compromise between the previous two options. So, you've gone all the way around the circle, what are you going to do?

Buying units that do not yet exist offers the most potential for financial reward. However, rewards like this don't come without risk. Buying an existing unit may mean settling for an older place to live, but you will have the benefits of seeing what you are getting. Both options have their appeal. Which one sounds best to you? Okay, I'll take the heat off of you and give you some general suggestions that may help to solve your confusion.

If I were an average person with a limited knowledge of real estate, I would retain the services of a buyer's broker. I would also hire a lawyer to work with me as I went through my homebuying adventure. Would I buy new or used housing? Frankly, I'd buy new housing, but most people will probably feel safer buying existing housing. And, in many cases, the purchase of an existing unit would be safer. Since the decision between new and used is so important, let's take a few minutes to run through the pros and cons of each type of purchase.

New Units

Buying new units in a condo or co-op development is nice. In some cases, the developer can customize the interior of the unit you're purchasing to suit your personal tastes and needs. This is a big advantage, and it makes you feel more like you are buying "your" home, rather than just a home in a tract development. It's often possible to pick the colors of your plumbing fixtures and kitchen appliances when you buy a unit that is either under construction, being converted, or scheduled for creation. Selecting your own floor coverings is another perk that often comes with the purchase of a new unit. There is a lot to be said for making a deal before a home is ready to move into.

Just as there are advantages to buying new units, there are also potential disadvantages. Construction and conversion jobs often take longer to complete than they were expected to. If you have given notice to move out of your existing rental, and your new home isn't ready for occupancy on the promised date, you have a problem. Are you going to live in a hotel for awhile? You might have to. Missed completion dates are common in developments. The problem is so common that you might want to allow an extra month to make sure that your unit will be ready.

Buildings that are being built or converted are generally sold with estimated expense numbers. It's impossible for a contractor or developer to tell you precisely what your utility costs or other expenses will be on a new unit. Until you move in and start living in your new home, your budget figures will have to remain guess-timates. You might be pleasantly surprised to find that the estimated expenses are higher than your actual costs. More likely, you will find that the projected expenses are lower than the true costs. Keep this in mind when you are budgeting your money.

When you buy a home from blueprints and scaled models, you may not get what you think you are getting. This is not to say that the contractor will have cheated you. Many people can't envision living space that is drawn or scaled out. Until the real walls go up, you might have a lot of trouble putting your new home into perspective. Experienced builders and few other people can see a blueprint for what it will eventually become. Most people, however, can't. It is best, when possible, to walk through full-size, model homes before committing to the purchase of a new unit.

One benefit of a new home is that it usually comes with a warranty that you don't get on a used home. A one-year warranty is typical, but some builders offer ten-year warranties. Getting a long warranty period is always advantageous. It's nice to have a warranty, but you may find that it comes into play quicker than you would think. A lot of new construction and remodeling has flaws that show up within the first year, sometimes within the first week, of occupancy. For example, compression fittings on plumbing valves that are found under fixtures frequently begin to leak after some usage. This is not normally a big deal, but it is something that you have to look for from time to time. Fixing such a leak is only a matter of tightening a nut, but letting the leak go undetected can do a lot of damage.

Carpenters, plumbers, electricians, and other trades-people make mistakes from time to time. Sometimes a door won't latch properly. A light fixture might be loose and wiggle when an upstairs neighbor walks. You might find air bubbles in your new vinyl flooring. Problems of this nature are common in new units. Most builders and developers will respond to your repair requests. They may not do it promptly, but generally, they will not put you off too long. While the work should be covered under your warranty, you are still inconvenienced by the work activity in your new home.

One of the biggest risks of being an early buyer in a development is that the development might never be finished. If this happens, you are in a world of trouble. Developers sometimes go bankrupt. Even if you do exhaustive research to choose a financially solvent developer, you could still wind up in a stalled development. There is no sure way to eliminate this risk. Most developments do see completion, but you must be aware of potential for financial failure.

Used Units

There are certain advantages to buying used units. For one thing, you can see exactly what you are buying. This may be the single most important advantage. Another benefit you gain with a used unit is that all of the bugs should have been worked out of it. I'm talking about construction flaws, not the type of bugs that crawl. Being able to track the performance of an existing building is also advantageous to you.

Are there more risks of maintenance expense with a used building? Probably. Any older building is more likely to need attention than a new building. However, some new buildings develop maintenance problems early on. The big advantage to the new building is the warranty period. You don't usually get a warranty when you buy an older unit. It's a good idea to have a reputable building inspector go over any building into which you are buying. New or used, you should hire an inspector of your choosing to verify the condition of your unit and other elements of the development for which you may wind up paying.

Aside from deferred maintenance and a shorter useful life, there are not many other disadvantages to buying an existing unit. One other concern is the fact that used units don't normally have the potential for a rapid equity gain. New units, if you buy into a development early, do frequently climb quickly in value. Used units usually cost less than comparable new units, but this is not always the case. You may get purchasing incentives with a new unit that you won't get with older units. All in all, there are not many good reasons to avoid solid, older units.

The ultimate decision of whether to buy new or used is yours. Consider your personality, your goals, and your desires. Make lists to help you conquer the question of new versus used. Take this same approach towards deciding whether to deal with developers or private sellers. Give some serious consideration to the benefits a buyer's broker can offer you. Take your time. Buying a home is a big decision, so give yourself the time you need and deserve to make a good decision. Now, turn the page to learn about inspecting, evaluating, and rating potential purchases.

CHAPTER 8

Inspecting, Evaluating and Rating Potential Purchases

Inspecting, evaluating, and rating potential purchases is an important part of your buying decision. Too much haste in any of these areas can result in disappointment. Failure to follow proper procedures before making a final commitment to purchase a unit can be very costly. And, as a condo or co-op buyer, you must pay attention to more than just the unit you are buying. This is something a lot of buyers don't realize. Suppose the tennis courts need new fencing and new surfaces? When this work is done, residents of the building will be paying for it. So, you have to look further than just your dwelling unit.

Inspecting buildings and mechanical systems is a job that is best left to professionals. Some sellers will provide you with inspection reports. Read them, but don't rely on them. Hire your own professional inspectors to make sure that the development you are buying into is not a ticking time bomb. It's always wise to have professionals perform inspections before you buy real estate, but it's very helpful if you can do some preliminary inspections yourself. This chapter gives you a short course in building and mechanical inspections. What you learn is not enough to replace the need for professional inspectors, but it is adequate to help you avoid some potential problems and lost money.

HOW TO EVALUATE CONDOS AND CO-OPS

Condos and co-ops are different from each other (with condos, owners get deed and own air space in the unit, whereas owners of co-ops own stock in a corporation), and they are both different from single-family, detached housing. Even if you have owned several homes in the past, you can't count on all of this experience to help you—unless you have owned condos or co-ops. For instance, the financing that you get for a co-op will be somewhat different from what you would get for a house, or even a condo. If you were buying a single-family, detached home with a half-acre lawn, you would be responsible for the entire half-acre. But, when you buy into a condo or a co-op, you will be partially responsible for all the grounds. Without question, you have to use slightly different procedures when inspecting condos and co-ops than you would with more traditional housing.

If the basement walls in a house leak, fixing the problem can be expensive. When basement walls leak on large buildings, like co-op buildings, the cost of repairs can be staggering. Would you normally think to inspect the foundation walls of a building where you were shopping for a condo or co-op unit? A lot of people wouldn't. You should be concerned about the condition of the roof over the co-op unit you are considering purchasing. If the roof has to be replaced and you own a co-op in the building, you will be paying part of the cost for repairs.

HIRING A PROFESSIONAL INSPECTOR

Some of what you look for when inspecting a condo or a co-op is very similar to what you would be watchful of in any type of residential real estate. But, the concept behind condos and co-ops places additional burdens on you. How much does it cost to have the trash picked up from the co-op building? Hey, you're going to be paying for some of the cost, so find out what to expect. How long will it be before all the balconies on the building will have to be repaired or replaced? I suggest you find out. Obviously, you probably don't have the expertise to see and recognize a lot of problems that might haunt you after your purchase. This is where a professional inspector is valuable. But, you can check to see if all the plumbing in the unit you are buying works. It doesn't take long to test the heating and cooling system for basic operation. A professional should come along behind you for a comprehensive check, but there is no point in paying an inspector to look at a building if you can rule a unit out on your own.

INSIDER TIP

It's a good idea to hire a professional property inspector to inspect the development into which you're considering buying. Since you will be responsible for a portion of the costs for maintenance and repairs, you have to inspect more than just your private unit. Have the entire property inspected.

Professional building and mechanical inspections are not cheap. They are usually worth every cent you spend, but you can expect to spend hundreds of dollars each time you have a building evaluated by a professional firm. The cost of inspections is high enough to warrant a little investigative work on your own. I don't feel that you should ever forego a professional inspection if you are close to buying a property. However, if you can determine that a building has enough problems in it to justify moving on to other buildings, there is no sense in paying hundreds of dollars for an inspection.

Doing Your Own Inspections

Do you have any mechanical ability? Have you ever worked in construction or remodeling? Even if you don't feel qualified in the least to inspect buildings on your own, don't rule yourself out automatically. There are many aspects of a building that almost anyone can inspect. By the time you finish this chapter, you will know what you can look into on your own. It doesn't take a master carpenter to figure out that doors won't latch or that cabinet doors are difficult to pull out and push in. Simple flaws might be all it takes to steer you toward another building.

If you call in professional inspectors for every building that you consider as a possible purchase, you could spend thousands of dollars before finding the home that is perfect for you. Hold off on the inspectors until you are extremely serious about buying a particular unit. Don't hesitate to call more than one inspection company. Some companies do full-scale inspections. Others specialize in one field, such as plumbing or heating, ventilation, and air-conditioning (HVAC) work. Depending upon the credentials of various inspection companies, you might find that you are better off to call in specialized companies for some, if not all, of your inspection needs. We will talk more about this shortly.

Using a Rating System

Most people who are looking for a new place to live spend a considerable amount of time in their search. They often visit numerous homes before making a buying decision. Sometimes it becomes difficult to remember details about various properties. Comparing and evaluating potential purchases is a task with which some people have trouble. I'm going to show you some professional techniques that will make the process easier and more enjoyable for you.

If you have a rating system to use during your property evaluations, you are less likely to become overwhelmed. A simple checklist can make a huge difference in how you go about your decision-making process. Checklists can be used from the moment you see a potential purchase to the time that you close your deal and move into your new home. You don't have to be a high-tech genius to make smart buys. A regular pencil and a pad of paper is all that you have to deal with when narrowing the field of prospective purchases. If you like using computers to run spreadsheets and to maintain databases, you can employ your computer in the selection process of your condo or co-op. As long as you know the basic principals, any type of record-keeping will do. This is a procedure that we will cover more closely later.

STEPS TO MAKING AN INFORMED PURCHASE

Let's go over the basic steps that you might take in buying your condo or co-op. We will assume that you are working with a buyer's broker who has lined up several units for you to take a look at. Your first walk-through will probably be one of general interest. Does the space seem adequate for your needs? Is the location good? Do you like the kitchen layout? Questions like these normally come first. After this walk-through, you may want to come back and look more closely at the unit. This time you are looking for details. Is the carpet badly worn? Do the windows work smoothly? Will your furniture fit in the living room? As you proceed through this stage, you should be taking notes. After looking at several properties it can become hard to remember which address has what amenities.

When you are shopping for a condo or co-op, you will have to consider many factors. Keeping good notes on each unit you see is important. Here's what you should take on your first inspection:

Items to Take with You for a First Inspection

- A notepad
- A pen or pencil
- A video recorder can be helpful, but this may be awkward on first inspection
- Most importantly, take an open mind

Once a unit passes the first two walk-throughs, you will probably leave to consider what you've seen. Another trip to the unit may follow. If the building passes your inspection, you might decide to make a formal offer to purchase the unit. Wait!, what about a professional inspection?

Items to Take with You for a Second Inspection

- A notepad
- A pen or pencil
- A flashlight
- A video recorder (if available)
- Comfortable clothes
- A tape measure
- A pre-prepared check list

Once you have satisfactory results on your personal inspections, you should evaluate and rate the unit at which you are looking. This step should be taken before hiring a professional inspection firm to go over the development. The evaluation process is simple. You compare the unit you are considering with other units that may be viable purchase opportunities for you. The evaluation is largely a matter of personal preference.

YOUR PERSONAL INSPECTION

Your first personal inspection of a unit is of great importance. It is what will likely sway you one way or another in your buying decision. A personal inspection is also essential if you don't want to spend hundreds of dollars for professional inspections on each unit you put under consideration for purchase. The initial inspection you make can be a casual walk-through. This is where you decide if the unit you are looking at appeals to you. Assuming that it does, you will need a few tools for your next inspection.

When you perform your second inspection, you should have a tape measure and a flashlight with you. Use the tape measure to get room dimensions. Write the measurements down on paper so that you can refer back to them later. The flashlight will be used to look under cabinets, in dark closets, and perhaps under the unit and in the attic. It's a good idea to wear clothing that is comfortable to move around in and that you are not concerned about getting dirty.

INSIDER TIP

Before you spend a lot of time going through individual living units, check out the grounds and common areas associated with the housing development. Some developments will not pass this first test. If this happens, you have not wasted any time on the inside of the buildings. But, if the common areas meet with your approval, move inside and go on a room-by-room inspection of the property. Some properties can be ruled out early. Having a strategy for inspection will help you save time and enjoy a more fruitful shopping experience.

Public Areas

Start your inspection with the grounds surrounding the development. Does the area have adequate lighting? Are the lights in good condition? How do the sidewalks and parking lots look? What amenities does the development offer, and what condition are they in? Is the general outside appearance of the development pleasing? How much parking is available to you? Move along with this type of questioning as you cover all aspects of the common areas and elements.

When you get inside the building, check out the hallways. If there is more than one building in the development, walk through the halls of all the buildings. Even though your unit is in one building, your dues will be used to maintain all buildings, so it's important to assess the condition of all structures. If the buildings have basements, take a look at them. Are the steps going into the basement solid and safe? Is there any sign of interior water damage, such as a waterline somewhere along the foundation wall.

While you are in the basement, check to see if mechanical equipment is sitting up on concrete blocks. Pay attention to storage areas to see if they are elevated. When fixtures and facilities are elevated, it's normally an indication of water problems. A flooded basement may not seem like a big deal to you, but it can be. Water can weaken a foundation and ruin expensive mechanical equipment. If this happens, you might get hit with a special assessment for repairs and replacements.

Inside the Unit

Once you are inside the unit you hope to buy, you need a plan. It's easy to overlook items if you are hoping not to find them. Emotions can run high when you are trying to buy a home. Establish a routine for all of your inspections. For example, start in the kitchen on each unit and then go to the bathrooms. From there, check out the bedrooms. Then move onto the living room, and so forth. You can do your inspection in any order that suits you, but it is less likely that you will miss something if you have a pattern that you work with. Let's do a room-by-room inspection on a hypothetical condo.

Kitchen

We are going to start our kitchen inspection with the flooring. The floor in this particular kitchen is vinyl. Is it in good shape? Does it curl at any point? Are there any bubbles in the vinyl. Can you see a shine on the flooring, or has it become dull after years of use? Check where the flooring meets the base cabinets to see that it is sealed well.

THINGS TO LOOK FOR IN A KITCHEN

- What is the condition of the flooring?
- Do all of the appliances work well?
- Are the appliances included in the proposed purchase price?
- Is there a garbage disposal?
- Does the refrigerator have an ice maker?
- Is the range fueled by electricity or gas?
- Do you like the cabinets and countertop?
- Are all elements of the cabinets in good repair?
- Is there adequate storage in the kitchen?
- Are there any plumbing problems?
- Do a complete inspection before you buy.

Kitchen appliances can look good and still fail to operate properly. If your unit is being sold with appliances, check each appliance to see that it works. Does the refrigerator have an ice maker? Is there a garbage disposal in the kitchen? Does the range use electricity or gas? Ask yourself these questions, as well as others, and make note of your findings.

Cabinets are always a big expense in a kitchen. Go through the cabinets completely. Open and close each and every door and drawer. Do the drawers slide easily? Are you able to get a good, solid seal on the cabinet doors when you close them? Are the shelves adjustable for various heights? How's the countertop? Does it have any cracks or burn marks? Is the kitchen sink caulked where it sits in the counter?

The walls and ceilings of any room are usually easy to inspect. All you have to do is look at them to see if they have aesthetic appeal. Check room openings and doors to make sure that they are up to par. Try electrical devices to see that they work. Use your flashlight to look under the kitchen sink. Are there any leaks or any evidence of previous leaks? The more you inspect, the less you are likely to get stuck with in the way of problems.

Bathrooms

Bathrooms in existing housing can harbor a number of problems. The list ranges from mold to dilapidated flooring. Does the bathroom have an operable window? Is there a ventilation fan? Will you encounter a moisture problem when using the shower? Do the tub and shower walls look watertight? Is grout missing from tiles along the walls or floors? Is the toilet solid, or does it wiggle when you try to move it? What does the piping look like under the lavatory? There is heat in the bathroom, isn't there? Do a complete and careful check of all bathrooms.

Some Things to Look for in a Bathroom

- Does the bathroom have a linen closet?
- In what condition is the flooring?
- Do all the plumbing fixtures drain well?
- Are there any plumbing leaks?
- Is the floor around the toilet solid?
- Does the bathroom have an operable window?
- Is the waterproof surround around the bathing unit in good condition?
- Can you see any sign of moisture damage?

Bedrooms

There's not a lot to look for in bedrooms. You must check walls and ceilings in all rooms. Flooring is another component that applies to every room of your unit. Bedroom floors don't normally get heavy traffic, so they tend to remain in good shape. Are there ceiling lights in the bedrooms? If there are no ceiling lights, is this a problem for you? A lot of new construction doesn't have ceiling lights. Switched outlets are used instead of ceiling fixtures as a cost-cutting technique for builders and developers. Closet space can be a big issue to consider when checking out bedrooms. Do the bedrooms have adequate closet space? Is the space lighted? Continue your checklist with this type of questioning.

Halls

Halls in condos and co-ops can take a beating. Heavy foot traffic is common in halls, and this tends to wear out carpeting and its padding. Can you see your footprint in the carpet when you pick your foot up? How long does it take for the footprint to disappear? You should be able to see an indentation when you step on most types of residential carpeting. Likewise, you should see the footprint disappear quickly if the padding is of a high quality and in good shape. Does the hall have good lighting? Many halls don't.

Living Rooms

Living rooms are often the rooms where the most money is spent on floor coverings and trim finishes. Does the living room in your proposed unit appear adequate in size and condition? If the room is large enough and in good repair, you should be all set. Even if the finish trim work is not as extensive as you would like, you can add to it.

Dining Rooms

Dining rooms, when they are available in condos and co-ops, are similar to living rooms. However, dining rooms often don't receive the traffic that a living room does. The walls and floors of dining rooms tend to stay in good condition for a long time. But, is there enough room for your china hutch? Can you fit your dining table in the room comfortably? Check every room in the unit.

Windows

Windows can become a sticky situation. Some windows are difficult to raise and lower. Check the windows to see if they stick during use. Are there enough windows to provide adequate natural light? How well insulated are the windows? Will the windows need to be painted, or are they vinyl-clad, maintenance free units? Are you starting to feel like a construction contractor? Hey, the more you check for yourself, the better off you are.

Heating and Cooling Systems

Heating and cooling systems can be expensive to repair. Check your proposed unit to see, first of all, if it has both central heating and air conditioning. Assuming that it does, test the systems. If you are buying an older unit, ask to see past maintenance records and utility costs. This may all seem like a lot to do, but it's in your best interest.

Plumbing

The mere mention of the word plumbing strikes fear into the hearts of many people. Plumbers are made out to be one of the highest paid groups of workers in the world. Although plumbers are not at the top of the income ladder, their services do not come cheap. This is a fact. You should try out all of the plumbing in your proposed purchase on your personal inspection. Flush the toilets. Ideally, ball up some toilet tissue and put it in the toilet bowls before you flush them. How long does it take to get hot water from the various faucets? The handles on the left of the faucets should control hot water, while the right-side handles should produce cold water. Is this the case? Some plumbers cross up their pipes by mistake, and a non-uniform piping arrangement could result in serious scalding with hot water.

Whenever you test the drains of sinks, tubs, and lavatories, you should test them under pressure. To do this, close the drain of the fixture, so that water will fill up in the bowl or tub. When the fixture is full, open the drain and allow the water to drain out. Does it go down the drain quickly? Can you see a tiny tornado being formed over the drain? If the water drains slowly, it can mean that the fixture is not vented properly. Another cause of the same symptom could be a drain that is partially obstructed. Remember to check washing-machine hook-ups, dishwashers, and other plumbing appliances and valves. Outside faucets are another consideration in the case of some units. Check all of the plumbing and make sure that it works to your satisfaction.

Top to Bottom

Essentially, you should go over your proposed unit from top to bottom. If you have an opportunity to inspect the attic of your building, do it. You might discover that the roof has been leaking. Black spots on the roof sheathing (normally plywood) will be a telltale sign of past leakage. Insect infestation is another major expense that can occur in a building. If you see small piles of sawdust in the attic of a building, you might be seeing evidence that a full fumigation will be in order, and structural repairs may be needed. This can get very expensive.

When you hire a professional inspection team, you should get a full report on the complete condition of the development you are investigating. This is good, but as I've already said, the inspections are costly. If you turn up obvious problems on your own, you won't have to go to the expense of hiring a professional firm to learn of the problems. Allow plenty of time for your personal inspection. Don't be afraid to ask questions of the seller or the brokers involved in the sale. Look into all aspects of the project. You're the one getting ready to part with some serious cash for a new place to live, so you have a right to know what you are buying.

CREATING A RATING SYSTEM

As you evaluate units, it is helpful to assign a rating to key elements and issues. Your checklist makes this an easy process.

Let's assume that there are three units in which you are very interested. By laying the three units out on paper in a side-by-side comparison, you can come to a fair conclusion of which unit is your first choice as a home.

Once the personal inspection, evaluation, and rating are done, you are ready to make a formal offer to purchase your unit. Remember to make provisions in your offer for a professional property inspection as a part of your willingness to buy. There are other contract elements that you should also have put into your offer. We will talk about the make-up of good purchase offers in the next chapter.

Assuming that your offer is accepted by the seller, you move onto the professional inspection stage. Once all of the contingencies in your contract have been removed, you will follow through with the full purchase procedure. Before you get to the financing and closing stage of a deal, you must have a deal to make. If you want to make a good deal, you have to be prepared to put some effort into the inspection and evaluation phases. Now that you know the basic procedures, let's get into some details that will help you along the way.

If you use a rating system when you are evaluating condos and co-ops, you will find that comparisons are easier to make. Depending upon how you go about your evaluation, a rating system can be worked into the program with very little effort. People are used to rating things on a scale of one to ten. If you are comfortable with this concept, use it as your rating system. Of course, you can assign some other type of rating. For example, you could use the words good, bad, fair, very good, and very bad to rate elements of homes you are looking into. As long as the rating system makes sense to you, that's all that matters.

You should assign a rating to every category that you evaluate. For example, you would create ratings for amenities, security, grounds, exterior building condition, interior common space, and so on. Once you do this, it's very easy to compare competing properties. Whether you have your checklists laid out on a table or on a computer screen, you can scan the ratings and see quickly how the buildings compare.

For a rating system to be worth its maximum value, you must be consistent in the ratings that you give. In other words, you have to have some sort of standard by which to assign a rating. This is difficult for some people to manage. However, the procedure is not complicated, and there is little reason why you can't be fairly consistent in your assessments. To expand on this, let's look at a few examples.

Rating a Kitchen

Rating a kitchen will be our first example of how simple a rating system can be to employ. In the interest of time, we will rate only the key elements of a kitchen. For your actual evaluation and rating, you should go into more detail than we do here.

We will start with the size and shape of the kitchen. On a scale of one to ten, this kitchen gets a seven for size and a five for shape. Why is this? The kitchen exceeds our minimum standard for size, but it is a galley-style kitchen, and we would prefer a U-shaped kitchen.

Moving to the kitchen flooring, we assign a rating of nine. The flooring is a high-quality, one-piece vinyl material, which is what we want. Why wouldn't we give this floor a full ten if it's what we want? Maybe we will find a flooring in another kitchen that we like better. By using the number nine as our top rating, except in exceptional cases, we have a code that makes sense and that gives us some flexibility.

The cabinets in the kitchen are abundant, but they are a very dark wood. We like the space available in the cabinets, and they are in good condition, but we don't like the color tone. Ah, we will use two ratings. For appearance, we will give the cabinets a rating of four. A rating of nine will be given under the heading of functional use. See how easy this is? You can create and modify your evaluation sheets and rating categories as needed. It is important, however, to make sure that all comparisons share the same categories.

The counter in the kitchen is exactly what we want, so we give it a nine. Plumbing in the kitchen is standard, so we give it a seven. Walls and ceilings are normal, so they get a seven. The appliances are better than average, so we give them an eight. Lighting is good, so we place an eight in that category. There is no window in the kitchen, and this is a disappointment. Due to the lack of a window, we rate the natural-light category for the kitchen with a one. By now, you should understand how easy a rating system is to use.

Consistency is the key to success in a rating system. Setting standards that you will use over and over is what makes a system work. To expedite the comparison of competing properties, you need to have identical categories for each building. If one building doesn't have what a certain category is set up for, place an N/A in the blank space to show that it is not applicable. But, keep all of your assessment forms identical in layout so that you can scan them quickly and effectively.

Let's say that you are considering five different units. Three of them are condos and two of them are co-ops. There will be some definitive differences between the two types of units. This is to be expected. Still, the rating sheets for all the units should contain identical categories. By doing this, you can lay the sheets out, side by side, and scan across the columns to see immediately what ratings were give for each building. This is a highly-effective way to do a quick and accurate comparison.

Rating a Bedroom

Rating a bedroom can seem like a difficult challenge, or it can seem too easy, depending upon your perspective. Bathrooms and kitchens have enough in them that the average person can see items to rate. Empty bedrooms appear barren. What's there to rate? Well, there's the walls, the ceiling, and the floor, but that's all, right? Wrong, there is much more to rate regarding bedrooms.

When you walk into a bedroom, you will probably know to rate the walls, the ceiling, and the floor. What else will you rate? Is there a ceiling fan? Will your furniture fit nicely into the space? Does the room have overhead lighting? Are electrical outlets where you need them? Does the heating or air-conditioning system conflict with your furniture placement? Are there any windows? Do you like the window placement? Does the window placement present security problems? Is there wiring for a telephone or cable television in the room? Do you have a good passage for escape in case of a fire? See, there really is a lot that you can rate in a bedroom!

Rating Every Room

Every room in the unit you are considering should be rated. Rooms that seem bleak, like bedrooms and dining rooms, still deserve a full rating. By doing the rating, you are doing more than what you might realize. As you move down your rating sheet, you are getting to know each room in each unit better. What looked good on first impulse may look different after you run your ratings. Filling out rating forms gives you some time to think, when you are not under the pressure of a professional salesperson. There are many benefits to using a rating system.

AFTER YOUR PERSONAL INSPECTION

After your personal inspection, you may have much information to sort through. If you don't, the inspection may not have been conclusive enough. When you inspect older, existing buildings, you should have a substantial list of considerations to think over. New buildings should not produce such large quantities of questions. Getting to the bottom of your evaluation is a chore that will require time, if done correctly. I'm not talking weeks or even days, but several hours should be allocated to the process.

OTHER CATEGORIES TO EVALUATE

When you get a report from a professional property inspector, included will be a detailed account of building and grounds conditions. Your personal inspection should produce a similar list of information. But, in addition to the structural aspects of your potential dwelling unit, your personal inspection will list many categories that a professional report would not. For example, is the school system that your children will attend, if they live in this unit, satisfactory? Professional appraisal reports often reveal information on shopping, schools, and other social elements, but building inspections don't normally go this far. Yet, all aspects of the unit you are considering must be taken into consideration for your personal evaluation.

SOME CONSIDERATIONS TO REVIEW BEFORE BUYING A HOME

- How is the local school system?
- Is the home located in an area that is going to grow in value?

- What is the local crime rate?
- How are the traffic patterns in the area?
- What types of amenities are available to you?
- Is there adequate parking for your needs?
- Does the development you are considering offer security services?
- Are the grounds around your perspective building in good shape?
- How would you rate the exterior of the building?
- Is the interior common area comfortable, clean and accessible?

Schools

If you have children, or plan to have some later, the schools in your district will probably be of importance to you. Some schools are better than others. The difference between school systems in which your child will enroll could be determined by only a few city blocks. Imaginary lines are drawn that show where children from various neighborhoods will attend school. If the school issue is of importance to you, make sure that you have a complete, clear understanding of what you are dealing with. Record this information on your evaluation form.

Location

Location is always a key element in the performance of real estate appreciation. Regardless of what type of home you are buying, you must always take the location into consideration. Real estate values are affected by comparable properties in the vicinity. The best home in the neighborhood is not likely to grow in value as quickly as an average home in the same community. It is very possible to over-build in a neighborhood. This happens with detached homes, and it can happen with condos and co-ops.

What is *over-building?* It's when a builder or developer creates a property that is much larger or much nicer than surrounding properties. The existing properties keep the value of the nicer property lower than what it's owner would like it to be. For example, if you were to build a two-story, colonial home that contained 3,500 square feet of living space, you would have a large home. If this house was built in a neighborhood where other homes of its type and size existed, the house should appraise for its full value. But, if the house is built in a community where other homes are of a Ranch style with about 1,200 square feet, the full value of the home will not likely be on an appraisal report. The large house would be considered over-built for the neighborhood.

When a developer does a condo or co-op conversion on an old apartment building, there are many options open to the developer. Wise developers will monitor local real estate and make sure that the conversion doesn't upgrade their buildings beyond a reasonable point. If a developer was to get carried away and add a host of amenities to a building in a sluggish part of town, the development would be likely to fail. Buyers might not be willing to pay the price for all the goodies. The building's value might not be recognized on an appraisal. This type of situation could result in the complete failure of the development, or at the very least, a considerable loss of money. It's possible for both condos and co-ops to be over-built.

Traffic Patterns

Traffic patterns are more important in some areas than in others. Where I live, in Maine, there are few traffic jams, and

RESEARCHING CRIME STATISTICS

The crime rates in local areas are often accessible public knowledge. I remember a time when I moved to a new state. It was a long time ago and I was young. While searching for a suitable place to live, I pulled up beside a parked police car and asked the officer if he would give me some examples of the best and worst places to live in the community. It worked in this case. The police officer was extremely helpful. This, however, may not always work. Don't worry, you can research local crime in other ways. Newspapers often publish crime statistics. You can ask a developer or a salesperson for statistics, but you may get a polished version of the truth. Do your own digging and find the facts. It will take some time, but it is a wise investment of your time.

rush-hour traffic is just a minor inconvenience. Around cities, such as Los Angeles and Washington, D.C., rush-hour traffic can be a major burden. Is the unit that you are considering purchasing in an area that will be commuter-friendly? If it's not, you might be better off to pay more for a unit in some other part of town.

When I lived in Northern Virginia, I often had to drive to the fringes of Washington, D.C. for my work. It could take me close to thirty minutes to move five miles. My total commute, even though the mileage was relatively low, could run well in excess of one hour. Figuring the time both ways, I might be wasting two hours a day on the road. Where I lived was cheaper than in-town properties, but I might have been better off to have moved into the larger part of the city and cut out the travel time. This is a potential problem that you will have to address on your own.

Traffic patterns, bus stops, and the proximity to train stations can all play a role in the value of a residence. Convenience comes with a price. Don't make yourself miserable for the next thirty years just to save a few thousand dollars in the cost of your condo or co-op. Evaluate the full situation. It may make a lot of sense to pay more now to have a better life for the time that you are in your new home.

Amenities

Amenities are nice, but are they worth paying for? Do you play tennis? Is swimming on your list of enjoyable pastimes? If you don't play tennis or swim, why would you want to pay for facilities that you won't use? A reason to pay extra for amenities that you could care less about, however, is that they generally pull in more residents. This helps a development to grow, and growth is normally good. Buildings that sell out quickly tend to go up in price. If you're one of the early buyers, you should benefit in the form of an equity gain.

Amenities, such as health spas, pools, and tennis courts require maintenance. Updating and upgrading are other typical costs associated with recreational amenities. As the owner of a condo or co-op, you will be paying for a portion of all the costs incurred towards amenities. If you buy into a building that doesn't offer amenities, your association dues should be less. This is just one more element of your total evaluation to consider.

Parking

If parking is a requirement of your living environment, evaluate this issue. How many parking spaces will you be assigned? What is the security situation around the parking lot? If you are buying in an area where snow is a frequent visitor in winter, how long will it be before your parking area is plowed? It will do you little good to have a car that is blocked into its parking spot with snow. Find out what the plowing schedule for the building is. If you need to get out to go to work, it's important to know that the snow-removal contractor will have the parking lot clear for you.

Security

Some developments have their own security teams. Many buildings offer some form of security. Does the public have unrestricted access to the hallways of the building you are evaluating? Does anyone monitor security cameras for the building? Is your individual unit protected with a security system? Find out as much as you can about security measures and use the information in your building evaluation.

Grounds

How are the grounds surrounding the building you are considering? Is there grass growing? Has it been cut recently? Are there any signs of soil erosion? Is the building fitted with gutters or other storm-water drainage? Refer to the notes you made during your inspection to recall your feelings towards the building grounds. This, too, is a part of the evaluation process.

Exterior of the Building

Is the exterior of the building in good repair? What type of siding does the building have? Will the siding need painting in the near future, or is it a maintenance-free material? Were the windows caulked when you looked at them? Did you see anything about the exterior of the building that bothered you?

Interior Common Space

What notes do you have on the interior common space? Is the lighting in the hallways adequate? Will the hall require new carpeting soon? Does the building have a lobby area? What did you like most about the common space? Do you recall anything that you disliked about the common space? Does the access to your proposed unit feel comfortable?

FINALLY, YOUR UNIT

When you evaluate all aspects of your potential unit, take everything into consideration. How is the traffic flow between rooms? Do you get a balcony or a deck to use privately? Are the bathrooms to your liking? Go through your list of notes for the individual unit and break out what is good and bad. Probe deep into your list and your memory. Did the kitchen have good natural lighting? Are the bedrooms large enough to accommodate your furniture? Did you visualize your belongings in the various rooms as you inspected them? Really put some time into this phase of the evaluation.

The unit you purchase now is going to be your home. It may be your home for decades. Selling a unit that you have recently purchased can be difficult. It's very likely that you will lose money if you have to sell soon after buying. This makes it essential for you to buy the right unit the first time. The effort you put into inspections, evaluations, and ratings will be rewarded with the happiness of buying the best unit for your needs and desires.

At some point, you will become comfortable with one unit. This will be the home of your future. When this happens, you have to start the serious steps of buying the unit. What you've been doing up till now might have been fun and exciting. The job in front of you can be frustrating, frightening, and disappointing. It is time for you to negotiate a purchase price. Unless you are willing to pay the full asking price, you may not be able to convince the seller to accept your terms. This could be devastating if you have fallen in love with "your" unit.

Not only are you going to have to negotiate a sales price, but there will be many terms and conditions that you should have inserted in your contract to purchase. Any one of these contract elements could be a roadblock to getting what you want.

It is common for purchase offers to be submitted to sellers on a contingency basis. Essentially, you and the seller work out all of the details of a purchase, and then you have some time to accomplish tasks described in the purchase offer. For example, you may have 14 days within which to have the building inspected and approved. If you are not satisfied with the inspection results, you can cancel your offer to purchase, assuming that you have such a clause in the offer you submit to a seller.

Contingency clauses are good for many reasons. In the case of inspections, you can avoid paying for a costly inspection until you know that all offer negotiation points on your offer have been accepted. It would be silly to pay for a complete building inspection and then find out that you and the seller couldn't come to purchase terms. Your broker or attorney can explain how contingency clauses work. The next chapter also gives you more information about contracts and clauses.

But, without the clauses, you could be at unreasonable risk. The next stage of your condo or co-op buying process can get rocky. Fortunately, the next chapter will prepare you for what is to come and will help you to find a balance point in the purchase process. Let's go to Chapter 9 now to explore what's in front of you as a willing buyer of a condo or co-op.

Chapter 9

Negotiating and Contracting the Purchase

Negotiating and contracting the purchase of a condo or co-op is a big step, and it's a lot of responsibility to put upon yourself. Stress levels can run high when you are trying to drive a bargain for a new home. Emotions often get in the way of rational thinking for new home buyers. If you are not careful, you can put yourself in an undesirable position. Guidance from an experienced buyer's broker or real estate attorney is one of your best defenses against the trauma that some new buyers suffer.

Buying a new home should be fun. It should be exciting. Many people never make a larger investment than in the home in which they live. Their homes might be their only hedge against inflation. Retirements sometimes depend upon the purchase of a home. There is a lot at stake when you decide to sign your name on a mortgage loan. Does the process of buying a home live up to the expectations of most buyers? I don't think so. Based on my extensive experience as a broker and a builder, I'd say that most buyers, especially first-time buyers, bite off much more than they expect to chew.

Buying a new home should be fun and exciting. Unfortunately, the process can become almost like a financial war, and the conflicts between parties to the transactions can run rampant. There is some good news. You can limit the frustration and the problems of buying a home if you know how to handle the situation properly. If you have experienced guidance, by either a broker or an attorney, you will get into your new home with few scrapes and bruises. But, if the people you rely on are not top-notch, you might resent having ever thought of buying a home of your own.

Am I depressing you? Are you scared? It's not my intent to turn you off on the idea of home ownership. However, it would be improper for me not to make you aware of the risks and aggravations that you may encounter along your road to becoming a homeowner. Looking back over the decades of my experience in real estate, I can recall many happy home buyers. A mental picture of a lot of disgruntled buyers also comes to mind. What makes the difference between happiness and disgust? Many factors play a role in the determination of how real estate deals turn out. You are going to learn about them in this chapter.

Statistics show that many buyers of condos and co-ops are first-time buyers. Typically, first-time buyers are optimistic and naive. Without the right help, these people can wind up in what seems like a never-ending battle to get into a home of their own. It doesn't have to be this way. An average person can negotiate the purchase of a property with successful results. I strongly recommend the assistance of legal counsel and a buyer's broker, but you can do the whole deal on your own and have it turn out okay—if you know what you're doing.

What could go wrong once you decide that a particular property is the one you want to buy? You know the asking price, and the seller wants to sell, so what could happen? There is a lot that can go sour in the purchase process. An average individual can do a deal without professional help, but the odds of a happy ending are not good. Real estate is a complex subject. There are many laws pertaining to contracts and sales. If you are not educated in the finer points of contract language and closing procedures, you can find yourself in something of a maze.

Am I saying that you should never act in your own interest, without professional help, when buying real estate? In a nutshell, yes. You can probably effect a purchase, but it's doubtful that you can do it as well as you would with professional assistance. You have rights and remedies as a buyer, but if you don't know what they are, they can't do you much good.

This chapter is going to show you the mechanics of negotiating and contracting the transfer of real estate. However, it is not a replacement for qualified, professional help. Again, I urge you to seek assistance from both a buyer's broker and an attorney. Use the information you learn here to understand what is going on, but don't take it upon yourself to structure your own deal alone. Knowledge is always a stepping stone to success. However, without a complete understanding of what you know, you can put yourself in jeopardy. Allow professionals to help you. The money you spend for their advice will be much less than what you might lose without their words of wisdom.

NEGOTIATING THE PRICE

Paying full price for a condo or co-op is usually not necessary. There are, of course, exceptions to the rule. However, most sellers choose a selling price that gives them some room to lower. If the price is not lowered, some other type of compensation can often be negotiated, such as having a seller pay a portion of your closing costs or points. The most difficult prices to get lowered are the ones that are attached to new units. You can almost always get the seller of a used unit to accept a lower price; but you may have to work for your discount. The process is not always as simple as offering a lower price. In fact, this can offend some sellers to a point where you will have a very difficult time buying the unit at any price. Negotiation is an art.

How to Lose: A Case History

Does it seem strange to you that a seller might refuse to accept any offer you make? Well, I've heard of situations where this was the case. One property in particular, comes to mind. The building being sold was not a condo or a co-op, but what happened is a good example of what you should avoid, so it is applicable to condo and co-op situations. The prospective buyer in the deal was a want-to-be investor. He had read all the books on how to buy real estate with little or no money. Being hyped up on the books, he believed he could be the next major millionaire in the world of real estate.

He was trying to buy a multifamily building. His intent was to buy the building cheap, get government money to refurbish it, and then sell it. This was not a bad plan. The man came from Massachusetts to Maine to make his purchase. Driving a fancy car and wearing an expensive suit didn't improve his odds of getting a good deal on the building. But, it was his approach and attitude that did him in.

An elderly couple owned the building that was up for sale. It had been their home for many, many years. In reality, the building was in need of heavy-duty remodeling, but the owners saw their property as being a home, not an investment. The man from the big city didn't get in tune with the sellers. Instead, he started telling them what poor condition their "home" was in. He did this to justify a lower price, as many books tell you to do. The plan backfired on him. His arrogance and attack turned the sellers stone cold. They refused to take anything less than the listed price, and they were none too happy about taking that.

Knowing that he had made a mistake, the investor tried a different approach. He raised the amount of his offer and suggested that the sellers remain on in the building as managers. It wasn't a bad ploy, but it didn't work. The owners of the building had already made their assessment of the buyer, and they didn't want to sell to him. A good deal was lost by both parties. It was due to a poor approach on the part of the investor. When you are driving a hard bargain, you have to know what buttons to push and when to push them. One wrong move is all it takes to kill your chances for making a great deal.

Getting the asking price of a property lowered can be easy, but it usually require some tactful negotiation. If you are working with an experienced buyer's brokers, you have a coach in your corner. This is very beneficial. Brokers who are in the trenches every day, as I have been, know a lot more about the finer points of negotiation manipulation than the average home buyer does. If you are using a buyer's broker, listen to what the professional has to say. Draw your own conclusions, but listen carefully. The broker will probably be right more often than not.

How can you drive a hard bargain without alienating the seller? There are many ways to cut a good deal without getting cut out of the deal. It's usually considered safe to offer a lower price on a unit that is for sale, as long as the offer is not offensive. But, what is offensive? If you offer five percent less for a property than what is being asked for it, you shouldn't hurt anyone's feelings. Even a ten percent drop will probably keep you in the ball game. It's when you expect the seller to take a nose-dive that you are likely to be hurting yourself in the negotiations.

There is no set procedure for picking an asking price. Some people don't like to dicker. They put a price on their property that is non-negotiable. This, however, is unusual. If I were to guess, I'd say that most resale units are priced at least five percent above what the seller will take. This assumption is based on many years of negotiating experience, but don't carve it in stone.

As a listing broker, I've had sellers who wanted to jack their asking prices up to a point about twenty percent higher than average market rates. This is absurd. When I run into a seller like this, I refuse to list the property. It's a waste of my time and advertising money to pitch properties that are grossly inflated. When I list a property, I do a comparative market analysis (CMA). This compares comparable properties that have sold and closed in recent months. From this, I'm able to give sellers a realistic view of what they may receive from a sale. Your buyer's broker can do a CMA for you on any subject property and let you know what a realistic price is. This is a strong way to start your negotiations.

GETTING AN ASKING PRICE LOWERED

Getting an asking price lowered is usually easier if you can offer justification for your reduced offer. At the very least, it's less offensive to a seller when you can show viable reasons for offering a lower price. If a property is priced right and you want to buy it cheap, you've got a tough row to hoe. But, when a property is overpriced, you can probably get the sales figure driven down to an acceptable point. In fact, let's discuss, in detail, how you and your broker can work to accomplish this goal.

What types of reasons might be acceptable to sellers? Surprisingly, you don't have to have a lot of support for your reason to gain the acceptance of many sellers. Human ego is difficult to understand. But, if you give a person a favorable way to retreat, you can often emerge the victor. Give a seller some justification for taking a lower price, and you just might get a bargain. Talk to your broker, but basically, any reasonable objections you have to an asking price can help you lower the acquisition cost of your next home.

IS THE UNIT NEW OR USED?

The tactics used to lower a price are similar whether you are dealing with a new or used unit. However, it is generally easier to get prices lowered on used units. Sellers of new units are generally developers, builders, or investors. This group of sellers is

When you ask a seller to lower an asking price only because you want him or her to, you have less chance of success than you would if you could give the seller a better reason for your request. On the other hand, it rarely hurts to ask for a reduction in price, even if you don't have a particular reason. As long as your offer is not offensive, a seller will frequently either accept the offer or give you a counteroffer. The counter may still be at full price, but hey, you don't know unless you ask. Just remember this, don't insult a seller with a major lowball offer.

money-motivated, and it hurts their profit program to accept lower prices. Now this may be a little confusing, but pay attention, and you will understand what I'm saying. In fact, I'll give you an example.

Let's say that I'm a developer who has just started selling units in a 100-unit condo complex. My asking price is $175,000. Ideally, I'd like to get the full price, but I'm open to reasonable offers. However, I don't want any sale going on record below the $175,000 price. Well, how are you supposed to get a lower price if I'm unwilling to record a sale at a lower price? You ask for other concessions. For example, you might make a full-price offer, subject to me paying your moving costs, a portion of your closing costs, and a decorating allowance. Whoa!, wait a minute, what's going on?

As a developer, I want to keep my recorded prices high. This helps me on appraisals and on future sales. It also helps me to raise prices as I move through my development. I might kick in $5,000 to help you get settled in, but I don't want to sell my units for $170,000. Essentially, you pay full price, but you get a lot of money back in a usable way. You get a deal, and so do I. This type of approach is usually very effective with professional sellers, such as developers, builders, and investors.

CONTRACT FOR SALE OF REAL ESTATE

Contract made this ______ day of __________, 19____, at ____________________________, State of ___________, by and between ______________________________________(Seller) and_______________________________________(Purchaser). Seller hereby agrees to sell, and Purchaser hereby agrees to purchase, a certain lot or parcel of land with any building or improvements thereon (premises) situated in ______________ State of ________________, and described as follows:

____

____

The following items to be included in this sale:

____

____

Said premises shall be conveyed within _____ days from the date of this contract by a good and sufficient __________ deed or seller conveying good and merchantable title to the same free from all incumbrances, except existing easements, restrictions, conditions, and covenants of record, existing building and zoning laws, and usual and customary public utility easements servicing the premises, however, should the title prove defective, then the Seller shall have a reasonable time after due notice of such defect or defects to remedy the title, after which time, if such defect or defects are not corrected so that there is a merchantable title, then the purchaser may at their option, be relieved from all obligations hereunder and withdraw earnest money or deposits, if any.

PAGE 1 OF 4 INITIALS_____________________________

And for such deed and conveyance purchaser shall pay the sum of ______________________________dollars ($___________), payment to be made as follows:

1. $________________________ received of purchaser as earnest money in part payment on account for said lot or parcel of land with any buildings or improvements thereon and items included, if any. That___________________________________shall hold said earnest money or deposit and act as escrow agent until transfer of title; that__________________ days will be given for obtaining the Seller's acceptance; and in the event of the Seller's non-acceptance, this earnest money shall be promptly returned to Purchaser.

2. $________________________ to be paid at the time of delivery of the transfer deed in cash, or by certified, cashier's, bank, or treasurer's check. 3. For a total purchase price of $____ _________________________________($__________).

This contract is subject to following conditions:

____

____

____

____

____

____

____

____

PAGE 2 OF 4 INITIALS__________________________

Full possession of said premises shall be delivered to Purchaser at the time of the delivery of the transfer deed, said premises to be then in the same condition in which they now are, except in the case of new construction. New construction shall be completed according to attached plans and specifications and approved for occupancy by the local code enforcement officials. Reasonable use and wear of the buildings thereon are the only exception for existing buildings.

The following items will be pro-rated as of the date of the transfer of said deed:

Utilities, fuel, rents, real estate taxes for the current taxing period, for the town/city/county of ________________________. The risk of loss or damage to said premises by fire or otherwise until the transfer of title hereunder is assumed by the Seller. All covenants and agreements herein contained shall extend and be obligatory upon the heirs, personal representatives, and assigns of the respective parties. That in case of failure of purchaser to make either of the payments, or any part thereof, or to perform any of the covenants on its part made or entered into, this contract shall, at the option of the Seller, be terminated and Purchaser shall forfeit said earnest money; and the same shall be retained by Seller as liquidated damages and the escrow agent is hereby authorized by Purchaser to pay over to Seller the earnest money, if any.

This contract is also subject to a satisfactory water test, by a testing service approved by the State of __________________.

PAGE 3 OF 4 INITIALS__________________________

The results of said inspection must be conveyed to all parties within _________ days of the final acceptance of this contract. Cost of this test to be paid by ___________________________. If a broker is involved, Purchaser acknowledges that ___________________________ ___________________________ represents the Seller and Seller acknowledges that ___________________________represents the Purchaser.

Witness our hands and seals on the day and year first above written.

I/we hereby agree to purchase the above described premises at the price and upon the terms and conditions above set forth.

Witness	Date	Purchaser	Date
Witness	Date	Purchaser	Date

I/we hereby accept the offer and agree to deliver the above described premises at the price and upon the terms and conditions above set forth.

I/we further agree to pay ___________________________ a commission for his/her services herein, ____________ percent of the sale price.

Witness	Date	Purchaser	Date
Witness	Date	Purchaser	Date

PAGE 4 OF 4

Does what I've just shown you make sense? Real estate values for residential property are tied heavily to past sales. Comparable sales and their comparison make up a lot of what goes into determining the value of a residential property. A developer who has a complex to sell out will do much better giving rebates, if you want to call them that, than by selling at a lower price. If sales begin to get recorded at lower prices, the value of the development goes down. This is not what a developer wants. Any savvy buyer's broker will know this, so talk to your professional representative for advice on how to get more out of your purchase dollar when dealing with professional sellers.

Private sellers of used properties are much more likely to take an obvious drop in asking price than a professional seller is. People who are trying to sell their personal units are looking for a sale, and they probably don't care if a below-market price affects the value of surrounding units. Consequently, your negotiating procedures will probably differ between private sellers and professional sellers.

If you submit a purchase offer to an average private seller, you will normally do better to ask for a combination of a price reduction and assistance on closing costs. Typically, forget about moving expenses and decorating allowances. This type of move with a private seller could be volatile. Again, a seasoned buyer's broker can be invaluable in this type of situation. Your broker should know how to "read the room" and come up with a plan for lowering your cost to get into a particular property.

Remember that you don't have to get a lower price to lower your cost of acquisition. Expenses like moving, decorating, closing costs, points, and so forth, are all true expenses. If you reduce your out-of-pocket expenses in a deal, you are essentially reducing your acquisition cost. You have to be broad-minded and creative to get the best deals.

MAKE YOUR LOW OFFER COMPELLING

Giving a seller some reason to accept a lower price is usually more effective than simply submitting a low offer. If you have a reason for lowering your offering price, you look better and you give the seller an escape route for taking the lower price. Few sellers like to give ground without cause. You, and your broker, should work hard to establish reasons for a lower price before you make an offer.

A Realistic Approach to Defects

Some properties suffer from defects. This is usually a strong position to take when asking for a lower price. However, you have to be realistic. If, in your opinion, the light fixtures are outdated and ugly, you can ask for a lower price. Will you get what you want? Maybe, but don't count on it. By defects, I'm talking mostly about physical problems with a unit or building. For example, if the carpeting in a unit is worn out, this is a good reason to ask for a lower price. When you, or a professional property inspector, finds a material defect, you have grounds to offset the defect with a lower price. However, before you get too gung-ho on this, make sure that the asking price does not already reflect the defect. Some sellers take defects into consideration when they choose a selling price.

INSPECTION ADDENDUM

This addendum shall become an integral part of the purchase and sale agreement dated ____________________, between ____________________________________, Purchasers and ____________________________________, Sellers of the real property commonly known as ____________________.

Within ________ days of acceptance of the above mentioned contract the Purchaser shall order an inspection of the property located at ____________________________________, from a qualified representative of the Purchaser's choice at the Purchaser's own expense. This inspection shall include the items indicated and checked below:

_____ Roof
_____ Heating system
_____ Cooling system
_____ Foundation
_____ Plumbing
_____ Electrical
_____ Appliances
_____ Chimney
_____ Septic
_____ Well
_____ Code violations
_____ Drainage systems
_____Other:____________________________________

End of page 1, continued on page 2

In the event the Purchaser's are not satisfied with the inspection results they may void this contract if written notice is given to the Sellers by ______________________. Sellers agree to allow reasonable access to the property for the purpose of this inspection. Additional terms and conditions are as follows:

____

____

________________________		________________________	
Purchaser	Date	Seller	Date
________________________		________________________	
Purchaser	Date	Seller	Date

Whenever you have a valid objection to the condition of a property, you have a strong position in asking for a lower price. Be careful, however, not to offend a seller. If your offer tells a seller that a property is in horrible condition, you could be saying, basically, that the seller is living in that horrible condition.

Many sellers, especially older people, become quite comfortable in their homes and don't notice gradual deterioration. Some people see their home as being worth much more than the market value. Sentimental value can play a role in the asking price of a unit. To get around emotional pricing, you need good negotiation skills and a way with people. It can be done, but it should not be done callously.

A Quick Closing

If you are in a position to offer a seller a quick closing, you may have enough leverage for a lower price. Many real estate deals can take two months, or more, to close. This means that sellers don't get their money for months. If you have a pre-approved loan or cash on the hip and can close immediately, this is a good reason to ask for a lower price. Many sellers will respond favorably to this type of approach.

Bank Deals

Bank deals can produce some great prices for you. Lenders often have to foreclose on residential properties. When they do, they often sell the homes for less than market value. Sometimes the properties are put up for auction. This, however, is not always the case. Some lenders advertise their repossessions in local newspapers. If your broker is tied into the local loop, you should be able to get some advance notice on this type of deal. Lawyers, bankers, brokers, and other players often exchange information. If your broker is a player, you might get a great deal on a foreclosure. Don't expect to get a big price break off the asking price of a lender, but don't be afraid to ask for one.

Banks maintain what is often referred to as work-out officers. These are people who have to work out the mechanics of getting rid of unwanted properties. If your broker has a reputation with work-out officers, you might be in luck. And, you might be able to get a market-value property at an extreme discount just by making a straight offer. Most lenders don't like to linger with delinquent properties. It is usually the goal of a lender to liquidate as soon as possible. Obviously, banks like to get as much as they can for a property, but they will often accept low offers in exchange for a quick turn-over. This is definitely worth your time to investigate. Talk to some buyer's brokers and see if any of them have working relationships with work-out officers at lending institutions.

Put on Your Deadpan Face

A lack of emotion on your part is one of your best weapons to wield when seeking a lower asking price. Although you don't necessarily have to wear a poker face to make a super deal, it is important to control your emotions during the showing of a property.

Sellers are often present when potential buyers tour a property. Experienced sellers, like brokers and builders, can pick up on body language, comments, and expressions that indicate your interest in a property. Private sellers are not as skilled in doing this, but they can see obvious emotions. If you want to drive a hard bargain, you must not show any emotion during showings. If you show anything at all, make sure that it is something that can be used to drive a price down. For example, if you are looking at a kitchen, make a comment about how the cabinets are too dark or too light. Basically, set the stage for your future negotiations when you take your initial tour. This is often the hinge in a deal. Let me explain by giving you some examples.

Assume that I'm a private seller of a two-bedroom co-op. You and your broker come to tour my unit. During the walk-through, I overhear some of your comments. The ones that stick in my mind are the negative ones. For example, you said to your spouse that the bedrooms are small, the bathroom has tile instead of an easy-to-clean fiberglass tub surround, and the kitchen is dark. Here are three reasons for me to expect a low offer.

Now, suppose you let your emotions show? Maybe what I will hear is how large the living room is, how much storage space there is in the kitchen, and how the vaulted ceiling in the master bedroom is wonderful. Comments of this type lend me to expect a full-price offer. Can you see the difference? Your game face is a strong element in your power to drive for a lower price. Let me tell you a quick story that is right out of my real-life experience.

I knew a couple who were looking at a contemporary house on waterfront land. Based on the description we had of the home, it would be exactly what the couple wanted. The broker showing the house for the seller was tuned into the couple. As the prospective buyers went through the home, they made many comments that the seller's broker could hear. I'll share some of them with you, and you put yourself in the position of the seller.

The house had two wood stoves in it, which the buyers really liked. But, their comments didn't reflect this. In fact, the couple turned the tables quite effectively. They said, as well as I can remember, "Well, honey, I like the room, but the stove is going to be a hazard for the children." This was a direct hit with the seller's broker as a drawback. Then there was the kitchen comment, " The cabinets are awfully dark. I think we will have to replace or reface them." This was another stake in the heart for the selling broker.

When the couple saw the skylights, which they loved, they made negative comments about heat loss. The whole showing went this way. The couple was nearly expert at taking the wind out of the selling broker. With the front put on by the buying couple, it was easy to hit the seller with a low price. The seller's broker would relate all comments made by the couple to the seller, and this would reinforce the reasons for the low offer. If you can play this type of game, you can win big. Is it ethical? Well, that's questionable, but it is effective.

A LOW PRICE IS NOT THE ONLY WAY TO WIN

When you are buying a home, a low price is not the only way to win the negotiations. You've seen a little about having developers pay for expenses that you will incur as an alternative to lowering a price. This is effective, but there are other ways to get more for your money, without lowering a price. For example, how would you like to receive $200 a month for twelve months to use your unit as a model home? If a developer will take your old home in trade, will that make you happy? Are you willing to pay full price if you can get an interest rate that will make your payments lower than you were expecting? There are a number of ways to get creative in real estate, and it's time that we explore some of them.

Closing Costs

Closing costs and points can be an expensive part of buying a home. It's not unusual for these costs to run five percent of a home's sales price. In other words, a $200,000 condo might have $10,000 of closing costs and points associated with it. Even when the costs are only three percent, the amount is

$6,000. There can be thousands of dollars at stake with closing costs and points. Who's going to pay these expenses? Buyers are typically responsible for the costs. However, most lenders will allow sellers to pay a portion of the expenses for a buyer.

It is not uncommon for purchase offers to ask sellers to participate in paying closing costs and points. Experienced home sellers expect to be asked to pay closing costs and points. In fact, many builders and developers build a cash cushion into their asking price to help buyers with closing expenses. Some sellers advertise the fact that they will pay a part of your closing costs. Other sellers wait until they are asked to participate in the payment of closing fees. Be sure to ask.

Before you submit a purchase offer asking for closing assistance, find out how much assistance your lender will allow you to receive. Your broker may be able to help you on this issue, but the lender you are dealing with is the most dependable source of specific information on closing costs and points. It's important to find out how much a seller will be allowed to pay for you. Why ask for a seller to pay up to five percent if your lender will only allow the seller to pay up to three percent?

Appliances

Appliances are almost always a part of a home package, but they may not be. Technically, appliances are not part of the real property, so they don't have to convey in a sale. Seeing a range and refrigerator in a kitchen might make you assume that they come with the property. Don't make this assumption. Appliances that are not "built in" to a dwelling are considered chattel, not real property. It has become increasingly common for appliances to be passed along in the sale of a home, but make sure you address the issue in your purchase offer.

If you are trying to get a price lowered on a unit where appliances are not included, ask the seller to include appliances in exchange for a full-price offer. This is a back-door approach to lowering the asking price. Yes, you pay the full price, but you get appliances at no additional cost. Since appliances are not real property, they don't have any affect on appraisal figures, and this is what builders and developers will be most concerned with.

Model-Home Fees

An uncommon way to get your purchase price lowered is to offer your unit as a model home. This may sound strange, but I used to do deals of this nature with single-family homes. The procedure is simple. You buy a new home from a builder. In exchange for some form of compensation, you agree to allow the builder to show your unit, by appointment only, as a model home. This can be a win-win situation for both you and the builder. You get a break on the price of your unit, and the builder doesn't have to pay as much for a model home from which to sell.

When I did model-home agreements, I generally gave buyers $200 a month for one year in exchange for using their homes as models. This, of course, was $2,400 for the buyer, and it helped me. Basically, I did it to move more houses, but I did use the houses as models from time to time. Shaving $2,400 off the price of a new home doesn't seem like a lot. But, getting $200 a month to apply to your payment for the first year is pretty good.

The model-home approach will work only with builders or developers, and it may not work at all. Some developers have their three or four models in place and are not interested in cutting any deals for home showings. But, you can use this approach to give the developer a way to lower your cost without reducing the sales price. It might be well worth it to the developer to pay you a monthly premium for a year if it results in an immediate sale at full price. Hey, it's worth a try.

Offering Your Existing Home Trade

Will anyone take your existing home in trade for a condo or a co-op? The concept of trading in a home is foreign to most people. If we were talking about trading cars, you probably wouldn't blink. But, talk about trading homes, and a lot of eyebrows are raised. Don't rule out the possibility of trading your existing home on a different one. You might be able to trade with a private seller, a developer, or an investor. Let me give you an example of how the deal might work.

Let's say that you have been living in a large, single-family home. You are ready to downsize into a condo, but you have to sell your house. During your shopping, you've found a condo that you love. Its occupants are young and expecting their second child. The couple needs a larger place to live, and they would love to have a single-family, detached home. Hey!, there's a deal here. You have a house, and they have a condo. You both want to buy and sell, so do a deal. The two of you can make a trade and everyone will get what they want.

Another way that trades can work is with investors and developers. Let's say that an investor bought a block of six condos in a development before the condos were built. The investor wants to sell them for a tidy profit. You come along and want to buy one, but you have a house to sell. Just as farmers rotate their crops, real estate investors often roll over their portfolios. You may have a good chance of getting the investor to take your home in trade on the condo. Expect to lose some equity in doing this, but you might get a fast, easy deal.

If a developer will take your trade, you might get more than your present home is worth, in exchange for paying full price for your condo or co-op. The developer wants the development to succeed. Full-price sales are the best way to keep a development rolling and appreciating. Even if the developer has to take a loss on the home you trade in, it may be worth it to keep the development on track. Don't expect a lot of developers to take this approach, but some may.

Buy-Downs

Buy-downs on interest rates are a common sale strategy. Many developers and builders offer to buy down interest rates for anywhere from one to three years as a sales incentive. When a rate is bought down, the monthly payment of a buyer is kept lower. Since a lot of people buy more on payments than on price, this is a successful tactic. If you are negotiating on a property on which a buy-down is not being offered, you can ask for one in exchange for a full-price offer. Builders and developers will often agree to your terms in order to maintain full-price sales. Private sellers may not be quite as motivated. Your buyer's broker can be of assistance in structuring an offer of this type.

Moving Expenses

Moving expenses can run into the thousands of dollars. If you can get a seller to pay your moving expenses (as mentioned earlier in this chapter), you have effectively gotten a lower price on the property you're buying. It's not uncommon for professional sellers, like builders, to agree to all sorts of creative terms and conditions. Getting private sellers to play the game can be more difficult. But, if you have a seller who is hung up on an asking price, you can ask for the seller to pay your moving expenses as a trade-off for a full-price deal.

Decorating Allowances

In the old days, a decorating allowance was a way for builders to rebate a lot of money to buyers. Lenders have tightened the reins on this type of exchange, but decorating allowances can still be used. Many sellers used this type of allowance to help people who didn't have enough money saved to do a deal. This is what made banks nervous. However, if you have money for your down payment and closing costs, your bank is not likely to balk at the fact that you are getting a generous decorating allowance. Check with your lender, but as long as you are financially sound, I doubt if there will be any objection to a decorating allowance.

DECORATING ALLOWANCES

A decorating allowance is a sum of money offered to a home purchaser for the purpose of allowing the buyer to, in effcet, finance some of the cost required to make a house a home. The decorating allowance might be for drapes, curtains, area rugs, or whatever. In times past, builders and developers sometimes built in the value of a decorating allowance with computing a sales price to help buyers finance their homes with less personal savings. In other words, it used to be common for a decorating allowance to be used to pay for closing costs, points, and in some cases, part of a down payment. This practice is not so common today.

When a house sells, the sales price is recorded in public records. This is part of what appraisers use to value other properties. The recorded price doesn't reflect items like decorating allowances. In other words, I could sell you a $150,000 unit and give you $10,000 for decorating and still have a recorded sale of $150,000. As a developer, this serves my needs much better than selling you the unit for $140,000. Decorating allowances are old hat, but they work.

HOLDING PAPER

When real estate professionals talk about *holding paper,* they are referring to seller financing. Getting a seller to take back a second mortgage can make a big difference in the monthly payments you make on your purchase. Real estate investors rely heavily on second mortgages to make their deals work. You can make second mortgages work for you too.

Not every seller is in a position to hold paper. Unless the seller has a strong equity position, holding paper is not feasible. But, developers may have enough profit in a deal to make it worth taking back a second mortgage. This could be especially true if a developer is trying to jump-start a project. Private sellers generally need their money and are unwilling to offer any owner financing. Investors, however, will frequently hold paper for a price. Depending on the type of seller you are working with and the situation surrounding your unit, you might be able to use secondary financing as a tool to give you a price advantage.

GOING TO CONTRACT

Once you have done your negotiating, you will hopefully be going to contract. This is a very serious step. You should have the guidance of an attorney during this stage of your home buying. Even if you are working with a good broker, you should have an attorney review all documents before you sign them. Surprisingly, few people seek legal assistance when they are working with a broker. In my opinion, this is a mistake. Brokers know real estate, but they are not lawyers. Personally, I feel that you should be represented by both a buyer's broker and an attorney. You can buy property without either one of them, but I feel the risk is greater than the reward.

When you get involved with a purchase-and-sale agreement, you will see that each offer you make will contain similar information. For example, all offers to purchase will be dated. They will contain a legal description of the property being sold. Street addresses are not legal descriptions. A condo located at

43 Loon Drive may have a legal description of Lot 2, Block A, Section 4, Map 6. All purchase offers will contain an offered purchase price, an estimated closing day, and a description of any earnest-money deposit. Other information will deal with real estate taxes, pro-rated expenses, and so forth. Most of this information is boiler plated into fill-in-the-blank agreements used by brokers.

Almost all purchase offers contain a section where special clauses are inserted. These clauses can help you, and they can hurt you. We are going to talk about some common clauses for contracts, but don't take what is said as law. Talk to your attorney before you sign anything. Have your lawyer draft your purchase offer for you. If you have a broker fill out a purchase offer, have your lawyer review it before the offer is submitted. Any time a seller counters your offer, ask your lawyer to look over the revised offer. Real estate contracts don't come with recession periods. Once you sign a contract for real estate and it is delivered, you are committed. This is very serious business, so don't take it lightly.

Favorable Clauses

There are many favorable clauses that you can have inserted in your purchase offers. There is really no limit to what you might ask a seller to accept. However, just because you ask a seller for something doesn't mean that you will get it. For example, if you ask a seller to pay the cost of your buyer's broker, the seller might refuse. Many won't, but some might. Anytime that you offer a seller a purchase offer that is not in complete compliance with the listing requirements of a property you stand to be turned down. This does not mean that you should be afraid to ask for concessions.

Contingency Clauses

Contingency clauses are one of your best friends when buying real estate. Clauses of this type can cover a wide variety of topics. For example, your offer to purchase could be contingent on your obtaining satisfactory financing. If you don't get the loan you want, you don't have to follow through with the sale. This is a standard clause, but few sellers will accept the language of satisfactory financing. More often than not, you will have to spell out the terms of financing that will be acceptable to you. For example, you might make an offer contingent on your receiving a 30-year, fixed-rate loan with an interest rate not exceeding nine percent and points of no more than two, with a down payment of not more than five percent. A smart broker will advise a seller not to accept an ambiguous term, such as satisfactory, in a contract.

Contingency clauses can be used for a multitude of purposes. Basically, anything can be the subject of a contingency clause. The following form is an example of a typical contingency clause, but remember, they can come in many forms and for numerous reasons.

CONTINGENCY PURCHASE CLAUSE

This contingency purchase clause shall become an integral part of the purchase and sale agreement dated ________________, between ________________________________, Purchasers and ____________________________________, Sellers of the real property commonly known as ______________________.

The Sellers retain the right to continue to market their property for sale and to accept offers subject to the rights of the Purchaser in this agreement. Sellers may accept such an offer subject to Purchaser's rights and after giving Purchasers 72 hours from the time of notification to remove this contingency and agree to a definite settlement date with the Sellers. If the Purchaser can not perform to these specifications the Sellers may void the contract, return all deposit money held for Purchaser, and sell the property to another party. In the event the need for notification arises, the Purchaser may be notified by certified, return receipt mail at ____, and the Sellers may be notified at ______________________.

The date indicated on the return receipt as the day of receipt shall be the date of notification.

______________________	______________________
Purchaser Date	Seller Date
______________________	______________________
Purchaser Date	Seller Date

For what else can you use contingency clauses? Property inspections are often mentioned in contingency clauses. You might say that your offer is subject to a satisfactory property inspection, to be completed within 14 days of contract acceptance. Will the old satisfactory line work here? Maybe, but not with an experienced broker. Good brokers will have their sellers counter back with more specific language, such as a property inspection that does not reveal material defects in a quantity that will exceed a repair cost of $1,000.

As a buyer, you want your contingency clauses to be as broad as possible. Sellers want to narrow the focus of the clauses and hold your feet to the fire. A contingency clause is sometimes referred to as an escape clause. Sellers don't want you to escape, so they are likely to tighten your contract language whenever possible.

Contingency clauses can be used for anything that concerns you. If you want to establish past association fees, you can make an offer subject to your review and acceptance of past association fees. Most contingency clauses are tagged with expiration dates. This gives you a defined period of time to either remove the contingency and close on the deal or to void the deal. Talk to your broker and attorney for more information on what contingency clauses should be in your purchase offers.

Contingency clauses are intended to protect home buyers during a contract period. It is not uncommon for a sales contract to contain several contingency clauses. As the contingencies are addressed, they should be removed. For example, if the contingency is a pest-control inspection, once the inspection is done, the clause should be eliminated. This is done with contingency releases, like the one below.

CONTINGENCY RELEASE

This contingency release shall become an integral part of the purchase and sale agreement dated ____________________, between ______________________________, Purchasers and ____________________________________, Sellers of the real property commonly known as ____________________.

The following contingencies are hereby removed from the above mentioned contract:

____

____

____

____

____

____

____

____.

______________________	______________________
Purchaser Date	Seller Date
Purchaser Date	Seller Date

Conveyance Clauses

Conveyance clauses address the issue of what—in addition to the real property—conveys to you at closing. For example, do the window drapes convey with the sale, or does the seller maintain possession of them? Does the free-standing fireplace or stove convey? Will you get the range and refrigerator in the kitchen? Many things that people assume are part of a property are not. Personal property is known as chattel in real estate circles. Wood stoves, free-standing appliances, window dressings, and other accents are all considered chattel. In other words, what you see might not be what you get.

When you have a purchase offer prepared, don't leave anything to chance. Does the microwave oven convey? Will you get to keep the washer and dryer in the laundry room? Spell it all out. If you detail what chattel you expect to receive in a transaction, you will not be disappointed after closing your deal. Any reputable broker can help you with this issue, and so can your attorney.

Most real estate professionals use pre-printed, fill-in-the-blanks sales contracts. When this is done there is not always adequate space to cover all important topics. This is where the use of addendums comes into place. An addendum can be used as an integral part of a contract. Here's an example of an addendum form.

REAL ESTATE PURCHASE AND SALE ADDENDUM

This addendum is an integral part of the purchase and sale agreement dated ________________, between the Purchasers, ____, and the Sellers, ____, for the real estate commonly known as ____________________. The undersigned parties hereby agree to the following:

____

____

____

____

____

____

____

____

____

____

____

____

____

____.

______________________________	______________________________
Seller Date	Purchaser Date
______________________________	______________________________
Seller Date	Purchaser Date

Earnest Money

Earnest money is usually applied to a purchase offer as a deposit. A lot of people think this is mandatory. It is not. A contract needs consideration to be valid, but it does not require cash. A promise for a promise is all the consideration required by law. But, a seller may not accept an offer that is without an earnest-money deposit. I've bought all sorts of real estate with deposits of $100. You don't have to fork over a full down-payment amount as a deposit, and I don't think you should. Whatever amount of money you supply as a deposit should be identified in your offer. Additionally, the offer should stipulate how the deposit will be handled and when and if you will get it back if the sale is not consummated.

PRO-RATED EXPENSES

You should have a clause in your purchase offer that deals with pro-rated expenses, such as taxes, fuel, or other expenses. Many boiler-plate contracts cover this issue, but you must make sure that your offer contains provisions for pro-rated expenses. In other words, if you are buying a property in June, you shouldn't have to pay the real estate taxes for the months prior to your ownership.

POTENTIALLY HARMFUL CLAUSES

There are some clauses in contracts for which you should watch out. They are not always bad, but they can be. Examples of potentially harmful clauses include but are not limited to time-is-of-the-essence clauses, owner-financing clauses, and bond-for-deed or installment-contract clauses. Rely on your lawyer to protect you in these matters.

Time-Is-Of-The-Essence Clauses

If a seller puts a time-is-of-the-essence clause in a contract, you had better comply with all terms of the agreement by or before the dates given in the agreement. Running past a closing date by just one hour can void a deal when a time-is-of-the-essence clause has been inserted. Unless you are positive that you can perform by contracted dates, don't sign any agreement that contains such a clause. You could lose your deposit and your contractual right to purchase the property if you are late in your performance.

Owner-Financing Clauses

Owner financing is something in which a lot of buyers are interested. Some owner financing is good, but there are types that are dangerous for you. If you agree to a large balloon payment on a second mortgage, you could lose your home if you can't cover the cost of the balloon payment when it's due. Balloon payments keep monthly payments low, but they also can be a ticking bomb waiting to go off.

Bond-For-Deed Clauses

Some sellers will finance a property to you on a bond for deed. This is also known as an installment contract. Doing business with this type of financing is very risky. You don't get title to the property until the full amount of the loan is paid. If you default, the seller may repossess the property. It's also possible that the seller will leverage the property for other deals and get you entangled in a major financial mess. For the most part, stay away from bond-for-deed financing.

We could go on and on with hypothetical clauses and situations. Because an entire book could be written solely on the subject of contract provisions, I can't fully prepare you for all the hooks that a seller might plant in a contract. You should, therefore, talk to your broker and attorney to determine exactly what you do and don't want in your purchase offers. Each individual has special needs and requirements, and I can't advise you personally without knowing all the facts pertaining to your personal situation. It is enough for you to know that there are options for you to take control of your offers. Armed with this knowledge, you can consult with your legal counsel to pinpoint your exact needs. It can't be repeated strongly or often enough: Always consult your attorney before signing any real estate agreement.

CHAPTER 10

Financing Factors

Financing can be one of the biggest factors in a successful home purchase. Very few people can afford to buy homes without the aid of financing. Fortunately, there is normally no shortage of mortgage money available to you. However, there can be so many sources for financing that choosing a lender can be difficult, And you can discover so many types of loans that you will not know which way to turn. Unless you are an experienced home buyer, a banker, or a broker, the various options for financing can be quite intimidating.

Should you get a fixed-rate loan? Do you know what an ARM or a SAM is? Who is Fannie Mae and Freddie Mac? What is the secondary market? How do portfolio loans work? What does FHA stand for? Are you eligible for a VA loan? How does negative amortization work? What does a broker who talks about loan caps mean? What is the minimal down-payment requirement for a home loan? These questions are probably making you think, and you may be confused by them. Don't worry, you will understand each of them soon. Home financing can be complicated, and finding the right loan is important. This chapter will help you make solid decisions in your financing options.

WHO CAN ADVISE YOU?

There are many types of professionals who can soften the sometimes harsh environment of home buying. Real estate brokers are common players in the process. Some of them are excellent, and others are not so good. It's important to find the right broker to work with, if you choose to work with one. Personally, I feel that most home buyers should work with an experienced buyer's broker. Lawyers can provide a host of valuable services during the process of home acquisition. You should seek an attorney who specializes in real estate. Few people can afford to buy a home without financing. This means dealing with lenders, and not all lenders are the same. Shopping or optimum financing can make the buying experience more enjoyable and less expensive. Do your homework and find these key professionals to work with early in your quest.

Real Estate Brokers

Real estate brokers can be a big help to you when it comes to financing questions. Brokers are not bankers, but they are generally aware of many types of financing programs and where financing can be obtained. At the very least, an experienced broker is a good place to start. Your broker can also give you some advice on which types of loan programs will best suit your needs. However, brokers should only be considered a step in the right direction. You owe it to yourself to explore all financing options before you commit to one.

Not all brokers are as up on financing as their competitors. However, to be really successful, brokers must have knowledge of financing and sources for funding. Few real estate deals work without financing. Many lenders send mailings to brokerages on a regular basis. These mailings pitch new financing plans and are aimed at bringing in business. The fact that the lenders who send these mailings are aggressive for new business may be beneficial to you. Some lenders are simply more agreeable to making loans than others. And, not all lenders enjoy making the same types of loans. For example, one bank might prefer car loans, second-mortgage loans, and construction loans over standard home mortgages. The next lender might view the market differently and cater almost exclusively to home mortgages. Your broker might be able to save you some time by suggesting a few good lenders for you to talk to.

Your Lawyer

Your lawyer may seem like a strange person to ask about financing, but don't discount this option. Real estate lawyers handle a lot of closing documents for house loans. This means that they see which lenders are doing a volume of business. Maybe your lawyer will give you the names of a few lenders to talk to. Getting leads on lenders is not the only role your lawyer could play in the financing of your home.

Loans and the terms that come with them can be quite confusing. Some loan packages have stipulations that may be detrimental to you and your circumstances. It's helpful to have your attorney review loan agreements prior to acceptance and closing. When you get to the closing table, you will be faced with a tall stack of documents to sign. It is your right to read everything before you sign it, but this can take an hour, or more. And, you probably won't understand some of what you are reading. Plus, if you want to close your deal, you have to sign the papers. See if your lawyer can get advance access to terms and conditions of the loan you are considering. By having your lawyer interpret the loan agreement in advance, you can feel comfortable at your closing.

THE CHICKEN OR THE EGG?

Which came first, the chicken or the egg? Well, I don't know, but I do have another question for you. When you want information on loans, which comes first, the loan or the lender?

Should you choose a specific type of lender to work with, or should you get information from several types of lenders? If you have enough time, get as much information from as many sources as possible.

> **AN IMPORTANT NOTE**
>
> Condo buyers will be dealing with typical home loans. When you buy a condo, the loan that you get is secured by real property with a deed issued in your name. This is the way most home loans are done. Co-op buyers, however, are not buying real property. They are buying stock in a corporation. Granted, the loan a co-op buyer gets can be similar to a home loan, but it will not be exactly the same.

Having confidence in your lender is important. You can start your search for a home loan with the bank where your financial accounts are kept. But, don't stop here. Some lenders don't offer the same programs that you can find at other lenders. Until you have reviewed all of your options, you should keep a clear head and keep your ink pen in your pocket.

TYPES OF LENDERS

There are many types of lenders who will consider offering you a home mortgage. Commercial banks are usually the types of lenders that most people think of when asked about home financing. Credit unions and savings and loans are also providers of home loans. Mortgage bankers and mortgage brokers are other options. Developers of projects may originate loans for their customers. Independent loan companies are other potential sources for a home mortgage. Gee, with so many choices, which type of lender should you talk to? Well, let's look at some of the differences between the various types of lenders.

Sources of Financing Funds

- Commercial Banks
- Credit Unions
- Savings and Loans
- Mortgage Bankers
- Mortgage Brokers
- Independent Loan Companies
- Builders and Developers
- Private Investors

Commercial Banks

Commercial banks are where many people go for a home loan. Ironically, this type of lender may not be as aggressive for home loans as some other types of lenders. Commercial banks can, and do, make home loans, but they also do a lot of other business. Is a commercial bank the best place to go for a loan? It could be. You have to check each lender's programs and compare them to your needs. Some banks are very competitive with other mortgage makers, and other banks charge a higher interest rate or more points than competitors. There is no way to make a blanket statement here. You have to investigate each lender personally.

Credit Unions

Credit unions often offer low-interest loans to their members. To become a member, you usually have to meet some form of criteria, such as living in a certain area, working for a certain employer, or working in a certain area. If you are a member of a credit union, it is worth checking the loan programs offered at the institution. Some credit unions operate on a more personal level then commercial banks. This, too, can be an advantage when seeking financing for your new home.

Savings and Loans

Savings and loans got a lot of bad press in past years. But, this type of lender is still a good choice for a home loan. Savings and loans tend to make a lot of loans for home purchases. The rates and programs offered by this type of lender can be quite favorable. I've had excellent results doing business with savings and loans over the years.

Mortgage Bankers

Mortgage bankers are specialists. They deal in mortgage loans exclusively. When you only do one thing in life, you usually get pretty good at it. Since mortgage bankers concentrate all of their efforts on mortgage loans, they seek and offer some of the most exciting financing packages available. The interest rates offered by mortgage bankers are usually lower than what you would find at some other types of lenders. Due to the specialized service and high volume of a mortgage banker, you can expect a better-than-average deal. However, a mortgage banker may not offer as much flexibility as you would find somewhere else.

Mortgage Brokers

Mortgage brokers are people who seek out financing for you at a price. Some mortgage brokers specialize in hard-to-finance people. Basically, a mortgage broker does all the leg work for you, and you pay for this service in the form of points or a flat retainer. Good mortgage brokers have a deep pool from which to pull financial resources. Many of the sources are of a type and location to which you would not normally have access. Personally, I would reserve mortgage brokers for a later choice and concentrate on more traditional lenders on a local level. Perhaps I should say a bit more about mortgage brokers.

Many mortgage brokers are upstanding business owners who provided a needed service for a reasonable fee. Some are not so reputable. It's not unusual for a broker to take a retainer fee up front. Sometimes you may be required to pay the broker even if financing is never arranged. It's very important that you understand every aspect of your agreement with a mortgage broker. Get your lawyer involved if you decide to work with a broker. It's very easy to lose a significant amount of money and wind up without a loan if you hook up with a bad broker.

Independent Loan Companies

Independent loan companies are sometimes a viable source of home financing. This type of lender is usually better known for second mortgages than first mortgages. However, some of the companies make all kinds of loans. Interest rates may be higher when dealing with this type of outfit. Some loan companies don't enjoy great reputations in the public eye, but others are just as dependable as any other type of lender. Overall, small loan companies are usually a more-expensive alternative for a first mortgage.

Builders and Developers

If you are buying into a new development, you might be able to arrange your financing directly with the builder or developer. In all likelihood, the seller will be acting as a go-between for you and a more traditional lender. Few builders or developers do full-scale financing on their own. However, many do work out deals with full-time lenders to offer buyers an attractive package that is originated through the seller. Some of these deals can be very good.

Builders and developers who are selling their own properties have a lot of motivation to get loans approved for customers. They will frequently offer incentives that make their programs very enticing. As with any type of loan agreement, have your lawyer review the paperwork thoroughly. Chances are that the offer will be legitimate, but don't take anything for granted.

PRIVATE INVESTORS

Private investors make money in a variety of ways. Some investors like to make mortgage loans. The loans might be sold or they may be kept in the investor's portfolio. This is much the same way that more traditional lenders work. A large number of lenders sell their loans on the secondary mortgage market. Private investors have the same option. My experience has shown that private investors tend to charge more points or a higher interest rate than what would be charged at a mortgage banker. But, the private sector is a possibility to consider. Personally, I would keep it low on my list of potential financiers.

A LOAN'S A LOAN, RIGHT?

A loan's a loan, right? How much difference can there be between different types of loans? The number of different types of loans available to home buyers can be staggering. Each loan can have its own little quirks and perks. To make the most out of home financing, you have to match a particular loan to your personal needs. You might find that a fixed-rate, 15-year loan will work best for you. On the other hand, a loan that offers an escalating, adjustable rate might be your best bet. If you have veteran benefits, a VA loan could be very good for you. There are so many variables possible with loans that it is practically impossible to discuss all of them in a book. However, we can cover the basics of common loans, and this will give you enough information to seek out more detailed information from various lenders.

Types of Loans

- Fixed-Rate Loans
- Adjustable-Rate Mortgages
- Convertible Adjustable-Rate Loans
- Reverse Amortization Loans
- Federal Housing Authority Loans
- Veteran's Administration Loans
- Portfolio Loans
- Balloon Loans
- Shared-Appreciation Loans

Fixed-Rate Loans

Fixed-rate loans are the old standby. This type of loan has been around for years and years. It is a proven performer of which most people are not afraid. The biggest benefit to a fixed-rate loan is that your monthly payment never goes up. You know right from the start what your last mortgage loan payment will be. There is peace of mind in this type of loan. So, a fixed-rate loan must be the best type of financing to get, right? Not in all cases. Many buyers can't qualify for a fixed-rate loan when they can qualify for an adjustable-rate-loan (ARM). If you are buying your condo or co-op as a stepping stone to a detached home, an ARM might be a much more effective type of financing for you. There are no cut-and-dried answers when it comes to financing your home. The circumstances surrounding you will dictate what is and isn't best.

Fixed-rate loans are generally considered the safest type of loan you can get, and they probably are. Since the payment never goes up, you don't find yourself facing higher monthly payments as the loan matures. You do, however, pay a price for this security. Due to the nature of fixed-rate loans, the interest rates charged on them is usually higher than what you can get with other types of loans.

When a lender makes a fixed-rate loan, the rate can never go up. This is a gamble for the lender. If prime interest rates go down, the lender wins and you lose. By this, I mean that the lender is making more money than expected on the loan and you are paying more than you would if your loan was tied to a floating market rate. But, if interest rates go up, as they often do, you win and the lender loses.

To protect their interests in loans, lenders usually speculate on the future of interest rates when setting a rate for a fixed-rate loan. To offset possible increases in rates, the lenders charge an interest rate for their loans that should average to a profit. Plus, they often charge borrowers points to originate the loan. Points are pre-paid interest that amount to one-percent of the loan amount for each point charged. In other words, if you were to borrow $200,000 and pay three points, the pre-paid interest charged would equal $6,000. This is money the lender collects up front in the way of interest, and you pay the remainder of your interest charges over time. This is one way that lenders make the most of fixed-rate gambles.

Under average conditions, I would say that fixed-rate loans are the safest type available to you. This is not to say that they are the best, only the safest. If you have a little gambling blood in your veins, some other types of loans may be of more interest and benefit to you. Were Mom and Dad wrong when they advised you to get a fixed-rate loan? Not really, but you have to decide for yourself which type of loan will give you the most advantages.

Adjustable-Rate Mortgages

Adjustable-rate mortgages (ARMs) are quite common today, even though they have suffered a good bit of bad press in years gone by. The name says it all about an ARM, the interest rate on the loan is adjusted periodically to reflect current market rates on interest charges. The adjustments are usually done annually, but may be done in more frequent intervals. When you get an ARM, you are playing the market and hoping to win with lower interest rates. Sometimes you can win, and other times you can get into trouble.

For now, we will concentrate on the mechanics of the loans. The major forms of mortgage loans and examples of how they work are discussed later in this chapter. When you get an ARM, your interest rate for the first few years is likely to be lower than what you would pay for a fixed-rate loan. For example, a starting rate on a fixed-rate loan might be ten percent, while the same rate on an ARM might be only seven percent. This makes a big difference in the amount of your monthly payment.

There are many variations of ARMs available to you. The best types have annual and lifetime caps. This means that the interest rate on the loan is limited in the amount that it can be adjusted. A common set of caps will call for a two-percent per year cap and a six-percent lifetime cap. Let's say that you get a loan that starts off at seven percent. At the end of your first year, the loan will be adjusted to reflect current market conditions. The interest rate on the loan can go up or down, depending upon the market.

Many ARMs go up, rather than down, but they can move in either direction. Assuming that your loan is a typical, two-and-six capped loan, your seven percent rate could go up to nine percent after the first year. You're still below the fixed-rate amount of ten percent. This means that your first year was very cheap and your second year will also be cheaper than fixed-rate financing. However, in your third year, the rate could go up to eleven percent. Now you are paying more than what a fixed-rate loan would cost you, but you had heavy savings in the first two years, and this offsets the increase in the third year. If you plan to sell your condo or co-op within three years to move up to a detached home, an ARM could be very advantageous. The risk to the ARM is that what started out at seven percent could wind up being thirteen percent during the bulk of the loan term. But remember, the rates could go down.

Convertible ARMS

Convertible ARMs can be changed from ARM status to fixed-rate status after a period of time. The time requirement is often one or two years. If you get a low starting rate on the ARM, you can play the odds and beat the cost of fixed-rate financing. A conversion fee is normally charged when an ARM is converted, but the amount of the charge is usually not excessive. This type of loan can be very good for people who are just getting started in home ownership or in jobs where their income is likely to increase annually.

Reverse Amortization

ARMs with reverse amortization look good at first glance but can haunt you in the future. With this type of loan, you could make mortgage payments for two years and wind up owing more money than you borrowed. I fell into this trap with one of my first homes. The loan I got had a very low interest rate, but when I wanted to sell my house, I found that I owed more on it than what I'd borrowed. ARMs with reverse amortization and no caps are what gave ARMs a bad name. Loans of this type can be dangerous, but not all ARMs are alike. Don't rule out ARMs as a viable alternative for your home financing. There are many occasions in which an ARM is ideal.

Federal Housing Authority Loans

Federal Housing Authority (FHA) loans can help a person make the move into a first home. These loans typically require a lower down payment than a conventional mortgage. It is also common for the qualifying criteria to obtain an FHA loan to be less stringent than what you would face with a conventional loan. Another advantage to an FHA loan is that you can often finance a portion of your closing costs.

FHA loans are very similar to conventional loans in the way that they work. You can talk with a loan officer to see what the exact differences are. Some real estate brokers, and even some bankers, don't like to deal with FHA programs. The paperwork that is involved can be somewhat more than what is required for a conventional loan. Personally, I feel that the benefits of an FHA loan outweighs any added inconvenience caused by the extra paperwork. You may find that an FHA loan doesn't suit your needs, but this type of financing might make the difference between getting approved for a loan or being told that you don't qualify.

Veteran's Administration Loans

Veteran's Administration (VA) loans require a borrower to be a qualified veteran of military service. If you have the background to be eligible for a VA loan, you can probably buy your new home without any down payment. That's right, no down payment. Sellers pay the points on VA loans. This saves you money in one sense, but the cost of the points is usually built into the price of the property you are buying.

VA loans are not much different from any other type of home loan once you have closed on the financing. There is more paperwork involved with a VA loan, and it can take longer to close this type of loan. My experience has shown that a VA loan tends to take about two weeks longer to close than a conventional loan. The big advantage to a VA loan is the fact that down payments are not always required. Of course, you have to qualify financially and as an eligible veteran to obtain a VA loan. Again, this type of loan could be your ticket to easy entry into a new home.

Portfolio Loans

Portfolio loans are loans that lenders don't sell. Many lenders sell a majority of the loans they make. This is a common practice. However, for a loan to be sold, the borrower has to meet certain requirements. The requirements for a loan that will be sold can be rigid. If you have had trouble with your credit rating, you may not be able to get approved for a loan that will be sold. But, if you can present a convincing case to a lender who keeps portfolio loans, you just might get approved. Since portfolio loans only have to meet the approval of the lender making the loan, and not the secondary mortgage market, you have more opportunity to smooth out rough spots from your past.

As a real estate broker, I've been able to arrange portfolio loans for people who would not have been approved for other types of loans. Most lenders and brokers don't play up portfolio loans, but many lenders do make them. If you have special circumstances that might be best served by a portfolio loan, you should ask lenders if they hold any of their loans. The fact that you find lenders who make portfolio loans does not guarantee you an approval, but it is one more avenue for you to investigate.

Other Types of Loans

There are other types of loans that we have not yet discussed. They are not used as often as the loans described previously. Balloon mortgages are loans where you do not normally reduce the principal amount owed until the time comes to pay the full amount of the loan. This type of loan is used more for second mortgages than it is for first mortgages. A balloon mortgage can be dangerous in the fact that you will be required to make a large payment at some point in time. If you are not able to make the payment, you will be in default and may lose your assets.

Shared-appreciation mortgages (SAMs) don't see much use in today's market. This is a loan where a lender or investor participates in the equity gain of your home. A SAM can put you in a position where you might have to refinance your home a few years down the road to pay your investor. Shared-equity loans work along similar lines to SAMs. In either case, you are basically using a partner to help you buy a home. This can be a good deal at times, but it can also be risky.

You can get into a variety of financing situations. Growing-equity mortgages are designed to help you pay off your loan quickly. Basically, your monthly payment will go up at regular intervals, at a set rate, to accomplish the goal. Wrap-around mortgages exist and can work to your advantage. Rollover mortgages are another possibility. To be fair to yourself, you need to sit down with qualified loan officers and explore all financing possibilities on your local level. Not all lenders offer all types of loans. This requires you to shop with more than one lender, but the time spent will probably be worthwhile.

HOW LARGE A LOAN DO YOU QUALIFY FOR?

How large a loan do you qualify for? The answer to this question depends on many variables. The qualifying ratios used for loans that will be sold on the secondary market are fairly standardized. Ratios for VA and FHA loans tend to be more complicated, but generally more liberal. Portfolio loans are negotiable to a point to which you and the lender agree. There are two basic, rule-of-thumb guidelines that are generally used when qualifying for a conventional loan. Conservative lenders use a 25/33 ratio, and liberal lenders use a 28/36 ratio. Keep in mind that lenders may use different ratios, so you need to check on your local level to determine exactly what you will qualify for.

Let's look at examples using the two qualifying ratios I've given you. With the information you are about to read, you will be able to do some rough figuring to see what you might qualify for. However, talk with a local broker or banker to determine your actual qualifying ability. Let's start with the 25/33 ratio.

Assume that your total household income, before taxes are taken out, is $75,000. You have two car payments that total $600. When you add up the minimum payments required on your credit cards, you have a total of $90. The rest of what you spend is for food, insurance, clothes, and other expenses that will not count against you in the qualifying ratios. Here's how to find out for what loan amount you may qualify. What is 25 percent of your gross income? It's $18,750. If we divide this by 12, we come up with a monthly figure of $1,562.50. This represents the amount of a monthly payment that you may qualify for. But, we still have to deal with the 33 percent. What is 33 percent of your gross income? It's $24,750. Divide this by 12, and you will get a figure of $2,062.50. This represent your total monthly allowance for a house payment, property taxes, and other installment debt, such as your cars and credit cards.

We know that the monthly cost of your installment debt is $690, so we take that away from the $2,062.50 and wind up with $1,372.50. Now we compare this number with the results of our 25 percent figure, which was $1,562.50. The lower of the two figures is for what you would be considered qualified. In other words, the total of your house payment and property taxes could not exceed $1,372.50

The 28/36 ratios work the same way, but they allow you a higher payment. Using the same income and expense figures, you would come up with $1,750 and $1,560. This means that you would be allowed $1,560 for your payment. A difference of $187.50 is substantial, so look for a lender who will use the more liberal ratios. Some lenders will bend the rules on ratios. You might be approved for more than what the ratios indicate. On the other hand, some lenders may be more restrictive and not allow you to go the full distance of the ratios. Until you meet with loan officers personally, you will not know exactly how much money you can borrow.

INTEREST RATES

Interest rates have a lot to do with how much your home will cost by the time it's paid for. The rates also play a major role in what your monthly payment will be and whether or not you will qualify for a loan. As an individual, you can't set your own interest rate. However, you might be able to talk a seller into buying down the interest rate on which your payments are based. Basically, the seller pays a lump sum to the lender in exchange for a lower interest rate. Not all sellers are willing to do this, but some will, and it's worth asking about.

How much difference does a couple of percentage points make in the amount of your monthly payment? Well, let's see.

Assume that you borrow $160,000 at eight percent interest. The loan has a 30 year term. Your monthly payment will be about $1,174.02. What would the payment be at an interest rate of ten percent? It would be about $1,404.12. The monthly difference between the two rates is $230.10. Obviously, interest rates are an important part of your home-buying decision.

You may be forced to consider an ARM instead of a fixed-rate mortgage. The reason for this is simple, the starting interest rates on ARMs are typically much lower than those of a fixed-rate loan. Depending upon your financial situation, you may find that you have to either accept an ARM or not be qualified for a home loan. This doesn't have to be a bad experience. I showed you earlier how ARMs can be advantageous. Since ARMs are an effective financing tool for people who are struggling with their finances, let's look at an example of how a typical ARM might work.

DANGER ALERT!

Beware of a loan that comes with negative amortization.

For our example, we will assume that the ARM is capped to be adjusted once a year. The maximum it can go up or down at each adjustment interval is two points, and the lifetime cap is six points. For the sake of our example, we will assume the worst and figure that the interest rate goes up by the maximum amount each time it is changed.

You have just borrowed $150,000 with an ARM on which the starting interest rate is eight percent. To keep this example simple, I'm going to use round numbers that are approximate. Your payments for the first year will be $1,100. The second year, your payments will be $1,300. By the end of your escalation period, your payments will be $1,777. Wow! Your payments have gone up by nearly $700 a month. Will your income go up enough to make this payment comfortable? This is the risk with an ARM.

Some ARMs are better than others. Have your loan officer explain all aspects of all loans to you. Then have your attorney review the terms and conditions before you accept any loan. What looks like a good deal today may turn into disaster a few years later. I'm not trying to turn you away from ARMs. Frankly, I think they are very good under many circumstances. However, it's important that you have a clear understanding of any potential risk that you may be putting on yourself.

YOUR DOWN PAYMENT

Your down payment can be one of the most difficult obstacles to overcome when trying to buy a new home. Making the payments on a home might not cost you anymore than what you are presently paying in rent. The tax advantages derived from home ownership make the effective cost of a home mortgage lower than what they appear to be. But, getting enough money put together for a down payment can be difficult.

How much money will you need for down payment? It depends on your credit history, the lender with which you are working, and the type of loan you decide to use. Typical down payments run from five to ten percent of the home's purchase price. Some types of loans, like FHA and VA loans, allow for a smaller down payment. And, there are times when a lender will ask for a twenty-percent down payment. In addition to the down payment, you will have to accumulate enough money for closing costs and points. It's not unusual for a lender to want you to have enough money for these expenses and to still have money left over in reserve.

What are your options if you can't put together a lot of cash? Try to get the seller to pay as much of your closing cost and points as your lender will allow. See if you can finance some of your closing costs and points. If you have blood relatives who will give you money for a down payment, you can go this route. However, the gift has to be a gift and not a loan in disguise. Sellers are not allowed to make your down payment for you when a loan is being sold on the secondary market. Some lenders might approve you for a portfolio loan without asking too many question about how your equity position is obtained, but don't count on this.

If you find an agreeable lender, you might have the seller hold a second mortgage in exchange for your down payment requirements. It takes a liberal lender to allow this, but some will. If you take this route, you will have two loans to pay off, and the second mortgage will probably come due much faster than your first mortgage. Don't extend yourself beyond your financial means.

I heard on the news last week that a new program is being put into place to help newlyweds with down payments. The program allows wedding gifts of money to be used in a down-payment fund. This is a new concept and I don't yet know all of the details, but you may want to ask your lenders about it.

TARNISHED CREDIT

A tarnished credit rating can be difficult to deal with when seeking financing for a new home. Lenders prefer to make loans to people who have good credit ratings. This doesn't mean, however, that your cause is hopeless if you've experienced some credit problems. The circumstances surrounding your past problems will have much to do with a lender's final decision.

Is it possible to get a home loan if you have filed for bankruptcy protection in the past? Yes, it is. Most lenders will consider making a loan to you if your bankruptcy was discharged at least two years ago and you've had good credit since filing the bankruptcy. People get into financial trouble for all sorts of reasons. If you have good documentation on why you got into trouble, you may be able to convince a lender to look beyond your credit report.

Let's assume that you were in a car accident three years ago. Due to the accident, you were disabled and had to file for bankruptcy. Once you recovered from the accident and got back to work, your credit has been clean. This is the type of situation in which a lender is likely to be willing to consider approving you for a loan. If, however, your credit problem was the result of poor planning, being lazy, or something along these lines, you're probably out of luck.

I've worked with a lot of buyers who have had varied backgrounds in their financial pictures. Some have had cars repossessed. Others have gone bankrupt. Many of these people have been able to obtain financing. Don't let a false assumption about your past credit history stop you from buying a home. Talk to lenders and find out what your options are. Maybe you will need a larger down payment. The lender may want written documentation that details your past problems. A simple letter might be all it takes to make a difference. Outstanding liens and judgments will almost always stop you in your tracks when applying for a loan, but past problems can often be worked around.

PERSISTENCE

Persistence may be needed to find financing for your new home. You may have to spend hours on the telephone and meet with many lenders before you find a program that best fits your needs. Buying a home is one of the largest investments you are likely to ever make, so take the time to do it right. You might walk into your local bank and leave with a good feeling right away, or you could spend weeks searching for a favorable mortgage. The key is to keep looking until you find what you want. Finding financing can be easy or difficult, but for most people, it is an essential step towards buying a home.

CHAPTER 11

Seeing Your Home as an Investment

Seeing your home as an investment may not be your first motivation in buying a condo or a co-op. People buy homes for many reasons, and your reason may not have much to do with investment potential. However, every home is an investment. Your perspective on a home can have a lot to do with what qualities you look for in the home. An investor who is buying a co-op or condo to use as rental property will examine all the investment angles. You might be more concerned about the color of the carpet than the financial returns possible with the property. This is natural and not unusual. But, if you learn to look at your home as more than a place to hang your hat, you should wind up with a better, brighter future.

People from all walks of life buy condos and co-ops. In some places, condos and co-ops are the only affordable housing available. I shudder to think what it might cost to have a custom, detached home built in New York City or the surrounding area. Therefore, availability and price are two reasons why people turn to condos and co-ops.

Young couples who are just getting started in life often look to small condos and co-ops as an affordable alternative to paying rent. Older couples who are looking to down-size often turn to condos and co-ops. Single people buy condos and co-ops. Investors buy co-ops and condos for rental property and to resell after a project is completed and prices have gone up. The demographics on buyers of condos and co-ops show a wide range of people.

Why are you considering buying a condo or co-op? What is your real reason for choosing this type of housing? Are you likely to need more living space in future years? Will the condo or co-op be a stepping stone to a detached home? You could ask yourself these questions for a long time and still have plenty more to ponder. The fact is, we can't predict the future very well. It is possible to make judgments on real estate based on historical data and current trends. You have some control over how your future will work out, but you can't control all elements of your life. Times change, and the changes can have a rippling effect.

When young people buy their first home, they often expect to live in it for a very long time. Some do, but most don't. It's common for people to sell their homes and move periodically. When I lived in Virginia, the turnover rate on homes was around three years. In other words, it was not unusual for people to sell their homes and move every three years. Yet, a lot of people swear that they aren't going to move for decades. Statistics indicate that most people will move several times during their lives. You may be the exception. If you are not, you had better consider the investment side of the home you purchase.

DETERMINING THE INVESTMENT POTENTIAL

What, exactly, is the investment potential of a condo or co-op? It varies with individual buildings. Generally, condos have more investment appeal and potential than co-ops. There are exceptions to this rule. In large cities, where co-ops are a typical way of life for the masses, co-ops enjoy good growth potential. But, if you look at averages, condos will usually rank higher than co-ops.

It is common for a condo to cost more than a co-op. Does this make the co-op a better deal? Not necessarily. The purchase price of a property does affect the investment return, but price isn't the only consideration. Sometimes what looks like a great deal turns out to be a mistake. You have to evaluate much more than just the purchase price of a property. We've already talked about associations and corporations that are involved with condos and co-ops. As a home buyer and investor, you have to weigh all aspects of your purchase. In this chapter, however, we are going to concentrate on some topics that you might not normally think to inquire about.

What to Look for in Investment Potential

- What are the past appreciation rates?
- Is the neighborhood declining, rising, or static?
- What is the past and present vacancy rate of the development?
- Will you be allowed to rent your unit at some time in the future if you choose to?
- How much are similar dwelling units renting for?
- What amenities does a development have to offer you?
- Can your new home benefit from improvements?
- Will your mortgage be assumable?
- How large is the development?

What Are the Past Appreciation Rates?

Past appreciation rates in an area can be a good barometer by which to judge future performance. Knowing how much real estate has appreciated in a given neighborhood is a key to making a good investment. There is no guarantee that future activity will reflect past performance, but it does more often than not. Checking past performance is pretty easy, and it's very easy if you are working with a broker who has access to previous multiple-listing books.

Whether you're buying an existing home or one that is being built or converted, you can benefit from doing a little detective work. If you do the investigating on your own, you will need to go to the municipal building where property transfers are kept. Real estate transactions are almost always recorded in a public records room. The information you can gain from scanning the documents is very valuable. Most of what you will be looking for is a property description, an address, and a sales price. All of this information should be available to you for any property transfer made and recorded.

Some people like to look through old newspaper advertising to find out what the real estate market was like. This is not a very accurate way to get your information. Asking prices in ads don't always reflect selling prices. The two best sources of information are the records room or comp books from a multiple-listing service (MLS). Most real estate agents have access to comp books, and they should be more than willing to run numbers for you. In fact, many places have computerized MLS records, and this makes the search much faster. Let me give you an example of how I would run the search for you.

Making an Appreciation Rate Search

Let's say that you want to buy a two-bedroom condo in Annandale, Virginia. The unit which you are interested in is an existing dwelling that is only a couple of years old. As your broker, I am happy to run a computer check on past sales. I would give the computer search parameters to pull up all condos sold in the Annandale area that share similarities with the unit in which you are interested. We might find that the most recent sale was made at $195,000. Then we could see that the year before, condos were going for an average sales price of $182,000. A few years back, the condos were selling for $149,000. What does this tell us?

We can see that in just one year, condos in the Annandale area appreciated at a rate of about seven percent. This is a strong appreciation rate. Anything at five percent or above is considered good in my book. When we look back further, we see that units in the area have enjoyed steady appreciation. This means that the unit you buy should go up in value as you live in it. As an investment, this is what you want your condo to do.

On the other hand, our background check revealed a stale market. If the condo prices had been fairly static, you might decide that the Annandale area is not the perfect place to buy a condo. Even worse, we might have seen that prices had declined. But, we would know all of this before you committed to a purchase. Can you see the advantage to looking at your home purchase as an investment?

A Strong Market Versus a Slow One

What is the difference between a strong market climb and a slow one? How much money is at stake over a five-year period? Well, let's stick with the Annandale example and throw in a slower market. The Annandale condo is going to be bought for $195,000 and appreciate at a rate of seven percent each year. The slower market will sell for $180,000 and appreciate at three percent per year. How will the difference play out in the end? Let's find out.

We will start with the slow market. Maybe you were drawn to it for its lower sales price. This would not be unusual. You invest $180,000 in a condo. It is your plan to sell it in five years to have a custom home built on a large lot. Here's what your five years will look like in terms of value:

Year 1: $180,000

Year 2: $185,400

Year 3: $190,962

Year 4: $196,690

Year 5: $202,591

I rounded the numbers off, but you make about $22,600 in equity for your five years of ownership. During this time, you've had a comfortable place to live, enjoyed tax advantages as a homeowner, and now you have built your investment up somewhat. How effective has your investment plan been? Let's say you are going to sell your unit at the $202,600 price. You will list it with a broker who charges a seven-percent sales commission. Assuming that you get a full-price offer, you will net $188,418. There will also be some closing costs associated with the sale. In reality, you haven't made much money from your investment. Depending on what you pay as a seller, you might net $7,000. Now let's see what the higher-priced property in the stronger market would have done.

The Annandale condo sold for $195,000. It had a seven-percent appreciation rate. You thought long and hard before buying it, because there were cheaper condos in other areas. But, due to your research, you decided to play the odds. How did you come out after five years. Here are the numbers:

Year 1: $195,000

Year 2: $208,650

Year 3: $223,255

Year 4: $238,883

Year 5: $255,600

Again, the numbers have been rounded, but they reflect an accurate pattern. If we assume the same sales condition for this unit as we did in the earlier example, your net, before closing costs, would be $42,712. This is a full $20,000 more than you would have made with the other unit. Which condo is the better deal? It's not the cheap one. But, the sales price was not the only factor. The appreciation rate is what made the difference. And, this is exactly why it is advantageous for you to determine appreciation rates in a neighborhood before you buy a condo or a co-op.

Which Way is the Neighborhood Going?

Which way is the neighborhood going? It is typical for real estate to rotate in cycles. Neighborhoods grow, they peak, and sometimes they bottom out. Declining neighborhoods are common, and you don't want to buy into this type of situation. Real estate investors have a motto. It goes like this: buy the worst house in the best neighborhood. Real estate professionals also have a motto. They say, "There are three critical factors in the value of a property; they are: location, location, and location." There are lessons to be learned from these sayings.

Savvy investors like to buy low-end properties in neighborhoods that are on the rebound. This is often where the fastest return on an investment is possible. If you can buy a marginal property in a growing community, the odds of that property's value going up quickly are good. If you bought the same property in a peaking development, the equity increase would be less likely. And, if you were unfortunate enough to buy it in a declining neighborhood, you would probably lose money.

The concept of where to buy is simple. Look for an area that has been down and is now coming up. Never buy the most expensive property in the development. You don't have to buy the bottom of the barrel, but don't go much higher than the mid-range properties. If you want to see a big increase in value, you have to leave some room for your unit to appreciate. When you start out at the top of the ladder, there are no rungs to climb. The more difficult part of this equation is rating the status of a development.

How can you know whether a development is growing, peaking, or declining? The work you do on appreciation rates will tell you much of what you need to know. If prices are stable or dropping, you probably shouldn't buy into the development. Visual clues are also worth noting. Look at the area. In what kind of physical condition is the building that you are considering? How do properties around the subject property stack up? Are the amenities, such as swimming pools and tennis courts, in good repair? Are the parking lots deteriorating? If the area looks good, it may be good, or it could be peaking. What does the surrounding area look like? Does your broker have any background information to share with you? The only way to find out what the status of a neighborhood is requires you to do research.

If you look at a condo and co-op and like it, you have the right to attempt a purchase of the property. You don't have to jump through the investor hoops. But, how are you going to feel if your new co-op is worth less two years from now than what you paid for it? The legwork that you do before you make a purchase will almost always pay off in the end.

How Many of the Units Are Vacant?

Are many of the units in the building where you will be buying vacant? A high vacancy rate in any project can be a serious financial problem. If the building that houses your condo or co-op is in trouble, you're in trouble. In an effort to fill vacancies, some developers will bend or change their rules. This can lead to problems in the property value. When there are not enough residents to carry the costs of routine operating and maintenance expenses, you could suffer from high special assessments.

It's usually advantageous to buy into a building early into its construction or conversion. Assuming that the project fills out as planned, the early buyers are the ones most likely to see increased property values. However, if the building falters and doesn't fill, the early buyers are the ones left holding the bag. There is a definite risk to buying into a new project. Buying an existing unit that has a track record offers more security, but less opportunity for rich rewards. You have to weigh this risk, and part of the process requires that you obtain reports on vacancy rates.

Can You Rent Your Unit to a Tenant?

Can you rent your unit to a tenant if the need or desire arises? When you buy your new home, renting it out to someone else may be the furthest thought from your mind. But, if you decide to move later in life, renting the unit to a tenant could be a wise move. If you buy a unit at a good price and get a fixed-rate mortgage, you could see a positive cash flow and some tax advantages from renting it. This might make a better investment than selling the condo or co-op. Some buildings frown on renting units to tenants. This is one of the questions you can have answered by having your attorney review the bylaws and rules of the building into which you are buying.

An investor who is buying a co-op to rent out will certainly confirm that the activity is acceptable. Typical home buyers may not. You should look for a unit where you have as much freedom as possible. If the project into which you buy is very restrictive, the rules could hurt you later. There are certain advantages to living in a building where tenants are discouraged. Usually, people who own their own homes take better care of them than tenants might. This, of course, is not always true, but it tends to prove true. Again, you are at a crossroads. Do you want to buy as an investor or as a homeowner? You have to make the call.

What Do Units Rent For?

If the building into which you are buying does contain tenants, what are the rental amounts for the units? How do the rents stack up against your mortgage expense? If your employer transfers you to a new location, would you be able to rent your unit out to cover your cost of ownership? Getting a positive cash flow from a condo or co-op when it has just recently been purchased is not easy. The same is true for detached homes. However, if you factor in the tax advantages, you may find that you are closer to a break-even point than what the numbers first indicate.

How can you establish rental amounts in your proposed building? Going door to door is not a good idea. Check ads in your local paper to see if any units are advertised in the building that you are considering. Call a few property management companies to see if they represent any units in the building. Talk with your broker. If you look hard enough and ask enough questions, you can find out just about anything you want to know.

What Amenities Are Offered?

We talked earlier about amenities. Having a health spa in or near your building may not mean much to you. You might consider a swimming pool a waste of money. Do you care if there is a recreation hall or a playground on the property? Amenities cost money, and this cost is passed along to buyers of condos and co-ops. If you don't need or want the amenities, why pay for them? Well, there is one reason why you might decide to pay more now—to make more money later.

Many people like amenities. If they didn't, developers wouldn't build them. When you are ready to sell or rent your unit to someone, the amenities might play an important role in your success and profit. Buying a unit in a bare-bones development is a cheap way to go, but it is not always the best way. Imagine how you will feel a few years from now when every prospective buyer who is looking at your unit declines to purchase it, because there are no amenities. How good are you going to feel about your cheap deal then?

Don't get me wrong. Amenities may not be worth paying for. This is yet another question that has to be answered on a local and personal level. In general, amenities are a good sales tool. You have to factor in the cost added to your unit when you buy it and the maintenance fees that you pay during your ownership. Will you recover this money when you sell? Doing your homework with the appreciation numbers should give you a good idea of what to expect. By now, you should be seeing that the research into appreciation is a very necessary process if you are looking at your home as an investment.

Will Improvements Improve Your Investment?

How will improvements that you make in your home affect its investment value? Some improvements are profitable, and others aren't. It's easy to see a higher return on improvements in detached homes than it is in condos and co-ops. Most condos and co-ops are built with similar materials and features. What you do to your personal unit might enhance its value, but the odds are against you. Can you add an additional bathroom? Probably not. Bathrooms are one of the best improvement values available to owners of detached homes, but space limitation in condos and co-ops can rule out the option. What if you remodel your kitchen? This could be a good move. Kitchen remodeling has a statistical record of a high return as a home improvement. You could tile your countertop, add appliances, upgrade your cabinets, or knock out a wall and enlarge your kitchen. This might pay off.

Generally speaking, I would advise against major improvements in a co-op, and I would think long and hard about them in a condo. Each property has to be evaluated on an individual level. Some condos are large enough to offer a lot of improvement possibilities. There is a lot that you can do with a co-op to make it more appealing than the surrounding units. Will you get your money back from such investments? You might, but you have to be careful about what you do and how you do it.

When you improve your unit, you could be putting yourself into the situation of owning the most expensive unit in the neighborhood. We've already discussed why being in this position is not good. If a majority of the units in your building are worth $150,000, you will have trouble getting $185,000 for your unit. Once you improve a place to a certain point, you start losing investment potential. The best investments are usually of average condition. They are not rundown, but neither are they top of the line. If you happen to have a penthouse co-op with an ocean view, the odds could change in your favor. But, fixing up an interior unit that has a view of the parking lot will probably be a big mistake.

Will Your Mortgage Be Assumable?

Will your mortgage be assumable? If you are looking to stack the deck in your favor as an investor, getting an assumable loan is one more card in your favor. Having an assumable loan with a good interest rate can make your success in selling your unit much more lucrative. You can take back a second mortgage, allow the buyer to assume your low-interest loan, and enjoy a profitable deal. Any edge you can gain is an advantage

Assumable loans are harder to come by than they used to be, but they still exist. In most cases, the person assuming the loan must meet certain financial requirements. Getting a blind assumable loan, one where anyone can take over the payments, is very difficult to do. The big advantage to having an assumable loan is that you may be able to offer a buyer a lower interest rate than what is available on the current market. By doing this, the buyer might pay you cash for the difference between the loan amount and the sales price, or you might hold a second mortgage for a portion of the difference. In either case, having the assumable loan available can attract buyers to which you would otherwise not have access.

How Large Is the Development?

How big is the development you are buying into? Does this make a difference? It can. There is usually safety in numbers. This is true in many situations, and it often holds true for condos and co-ops. Association fees are divided among property owners or stockholders. The more owners you have in your building, the lower your share of the expenses, at least this is the way it's supposed to work. To some extent, the theory does work.

If you buy into a development that has 200 units, you're in a fairly large project. Will your monthly fees be less than if you lived in a development that housed 100 units? Maybe, maybe not. When you add units to a development, you also add costs. It will take more tennis courts for 200 residents than it would for 100. More parking is needed when the number of housing units increases. The need for added common space and elements increases the cost of construction, operation, and maintenance. You are paying a portion of these costs in one way or another.

Would you be better off in a small development, say one that has 35 units? It depends on individual facts and your perspective. There are advantages to living in a small development. You will have a better opportunity to know all of your neighbors. When the number of people in a development is reduced, there is less noise to endure. The idea of living in a cozy, little development can seem very nice. And, the prospect of such a home can, indeed, be enjoyable.

Investors often prefer to own units in larger buildings and developments. Some of this may be out of habit. If an investor buys a small apartment building, it doesn't take long to find out that a six-unit building is usually a better investment than a duplex. The reasons for this are numerous, but one of them has to do with the number of rental units. If you own a duplex and one of your two tenants moves out, you lose half of your rental income. When a tenant moves out of a six-unit building, you are losing only one-sixth of your rental income. An occasional vacancy is not as large a financial burden when it occurs in a larger building. Some investors carry this line of thinking over to their purchase of condos and co-ops. Does it really make a difference whether you buy into a large or small development? It can, so let's look at the concept.

Assume that you buy into a development where there are 150 co-ops. Your cost of the corporate expenses is manageable, and you're happy. All of a sudden, eight of the residents stop paying their monthly fees. How much impact will this have on you? The eight residents who are not paying comprise about five percent of the development's population. Spreading a five-percent loss out over ninety-five percent of the stockholders shouldn't make a huge difference in your association fees. But, what would happen if the same number of people moved out of a development that contained only 32 units? All of a sudden twenty-five percent of the revenue would be missing. This is a much higher number, and there are only 24 residents left to pick up where the other eight left off. This could amount to a sizable increase in the demands on you for association fees, even if it were only for a short time.

Based on our example, you can see why many investors feel there is more safety in larger developments. This may be a false sense of security, but it's very real to a lot of investors. I can't tell you whether a small development is better or worse than a large one. Small developments are often easier to manage, and rules and bylaws are generally easier to change in smaller communities. Since there are fewer people involved, getting a consensus on votes can be faster. I don't know if there is a right or wrong answer to what size development into which you should buy. The question is, however, one that you should ask yourself.

Buying a home, of any kind, is a big investment and quite a commitment. You may see your new home as a dream-come-true, but you should look upon it with the eyes of an investor. This doesn't mean that you can't celebrate and decorate. All I'm saying is that you should, at least in the back of your mind, pay attention to details that may affect the future potential of your home. You can never be certain that there will not come a time when you must sell your home or convert it to rental property. Maybe you will live in your new place for the rest of your life, but the odds are against it. Enjoy what you buy, but make smart decisions along the way.

CHAPTER 12

When You Are Ready to Sell

When you are ready to sell your condo or co-op, you may find the task just as confusing as buying a unit. Some sales are simple, but many are not. To get the most out of the sale of your home, you must follow certain procedures. For example, if you did not examine the bylaws of your co-op agreement carefully, you might discover that the co-op board can exercise a right of refusal over your prospective buyers. This can be an ugly surprise when you are trying to sell your unit. Condo associations may hold a first-right-of-refusal on your unit. Condos are generally easier to sell than co-ops, and the boards for condos are usually not as restrictive when you are selling. But, this is just the tip of the iceberg.

Selling your condo or co-op might be easy, but what will you do if it isn't? Suppose you are trying to sell in a buyer's market; are you willing to take a low price for your unit? Do you have to settle for a low price, or are there ways for you to get more for your unit than other units? Will you use a real estate brokerage to sell your unit, or will you sell it yourself, to save the commission? These are just a few of the questions that come up when you prepare to sell your home.

I've been selling real estate of one type or another for over twenty years. Much of what I've sold has belonged to me, but I've also done a lot of business as a broker for others. Most recently, I've concentrated my efforts as a buyer's broker, but I've done countless deals as a seller and as a seller's broker. Through all of this experience, I've learned a lot. In a nutshell, I've learned that no two sales are alike. Some go fast and smoothly, while others seem to linger indefinitely. As the seller, you play a vital role in the sale of your home, even if you are having a brokerage sell the unit for you. If you don't cooperate with your brokerage, the chances of enjoying a fast, easy deal aren't good.

Many people have a false perception of the sale of a property. Few people who aren't in the business have any idea of the planning and work that goes into a lucrative sale. Making a sale can be easy, but making a very profitable sale takes more time and effort. From start to finish, the sale of a home can take from only a few weeks to many, many months. A number of factors come into play with a successful sale. We will talk about these factors, and much more as we move through this chapter.

SHOULD YOU SELL IT YOURSELF?

When you decide to sell your home, should you sell it yourself? Many people are tempted to sell their own property. They often resent the idea of paying a brokerage a commission for doing what some people consider very little work. There are times when brokers and brokerages make fast, easy money, but more often than not, they work hard for what they earn. Not only do brokers have to work for their pay, brokerages often invest quite a bit in advertising a property that is being offered for sale. With today's cost of advertising, you could spend thousands of dollars in advertising before your home was sold if you paid for the advertising yourself.

There is more to the question of selling your own home than saving the cost of a real estate commission. Real estate transactions can be quite complicated. Experienced brokers usually have a lot of training and take ongoing educational courses to augment their field experience. You probably don't possess this same type of knowledge. Yes, you could use an attorney to help you sell your home, but a lawyer is not an equivalent of an experienced broker. Attorneys make a nice addition to a broker, but you can't expect your lawyer to make the sale for you.

Are you capable of selling your own home? Perhaps, but how do you define the act of selling your home? If you are referring only to running ads in a newspaper, opening your door to strangers, and having your lawyer draw up a contract, you can probably handle the chore. However, if you are talking about selling in a way similar to those of professional brokers, you may have your hands full and wind up feeling overwhelmed. The job of selling a home for top dollar is not an easy one.

Some individuals do have what it takes to sell their own homes, and you may be one of these people. Generally, I would not recommend that an average homeowner attempt to sell a home without professional help from both a brokerage and an attorney. The money you think you are saving by doing this may not be nearly as much as your projections. To illustrate this, let's look at a quick example.

Assume that you have a co-op to sell and the market value of the property is $135,000. Further assume that local brokerages want between six and seven percent of the sales price as a sales commission. If you go with a six-percent brokerage, it will cost you $8,100 for the brokerage services, assuming that you get a full-price sale. Eight grand is a lot of money, and the brokerage may not be worth the cost in your mind. But, before you make a final decision, examine both sides of the issue.

If you list your home with the brokerage, you don't have to pay for any advertising. Your brokerage will screen prospective buyers and qualify them before showing them your unit. If the brokerage is a member of an MLS, and most are, your property will get a lot more exposure than what you could provide on a personal level. In all probability, you will see a faster sale when working with a brokerage, due to their connections, MLS, advertising budget, and sales force. You should consult an attorney even when you are represented by a brokerage, but the odds are that you won't require as many visits to your lawyer's office. When you factor in all the out-of-pocket costs that you will incur if you sell the home yourself, how much is the brokerage really costing you?

Advertising can be very expensive. There is no way for me to say how much you will have to advertise or how much the ads will cost in your hometown. You can run the numbers yourself. I can tell you, however, that brokerages often spend thousands of dollars a week to advertise their listings. I doubt if you are willing to compete with this type of a budget. Of course, the large ad budget covers several properties, not just yours. As a side note, there is another statistic of which you should be aware. It is far more often that an advertised property results in the sale of some other property than the sale of the advertised property when ads are placed by brokerages. This may seem strange, but it's often true.

The cost of time with an attorney doesn't come cheap. How much are you going to be spending every time you have a simple real estate question and call your attorney? This is an expense that you wouldn't have if you engaged a brokerage to sell your home.

So far, you can save some legal fees and all advertising expenses when you work with a broker. What else will you save? If you have to take time away from work to show your unit, you may be losing money. When you have a broker, you don't have to be present for showings. Not only does this save you time and maybe money, it often makes prospective buyers more comfortable when a homeowner is not present during a showing.

As an average homeowner, you don't have access to the MLS. This doesn't stop you from selling your own home, but it can prolong the sales period considerably. A big benefit to working with a brokerage, even though you are paying for it, is that you don't have total strangers walking through your home. If you open your door to anyone who responds to an ad, you could be putting yourself at risk of physical harm or property loss. It's sad to say, but true. Plus, you probably aren't going to screen prospects in a qualifying manner that will tell you if you are wasting your time or not. Good brokers will make sure that anyone who sees your home should be in a financial position to buy it.

SELLING THROUGH A BROKERAGE

Listing your home with a brokerage will probably cost more than if you sold the home yourself. But, when you consider all of the advantages that a brokerage can offer you, the sales commission may turn out to be much more of a bargain than what you first thought. There is a saying that tells you to get anything done right, you have to do it yourself. I believe in this saying, but there are times when it is not completely accurate. With a few exceptions, I feel that most people should list their homes with a brokerage when the time comes to sell. You should, however, be judicious in selecting the brokerage to which you commit.

CHOOSING A GOOD BROKERAGE

Choosing a good brokerage takes a little effort on your part. It is not as easy as calling the first company you see in your phone directory. When you list your home with a brokerage, you are making a commitment to the brokerage. In a fair transaction, the brokerage should make commitments to you, as well. As a seller, you are in the driver's seat. Brokerages need listings. In fact, they work extremely hard to get new listings. This, in itself, can be a bit of a problem for the inexperienced seller.

Instead of believing everything you hear, concentrate on what you can see in writing.

It is not unusual for brokerages to set listing quotas for their sales associates. In some brokerages, agents who don't meet their listing quotas have to look for new places of employment. This type of stress on an agent can lead to practices that may hurt you. There are many questions that should be answered before you sign a listing agreement with a brokerage. Let's go over some of them now.

Considerations When Selling Your Home with a Brokerage

- Choose your brokerage carefully.
- Ask for references who can tell you about past experiences with the brokerage.
- Make sure you and your broker set a fair sales price.
- Have your home appraised by a licensed real estate appraiser.
- Require your broker to provide you with a written marketing plan.
- Confirm what the average time to sell a property is with the various brokerages you are considering.
- Reserve the right to retract your listing if the brokerage doesn't perform in accordance with the written marketing plan.

Ask for References

Brokers and brokerages are quick to tell prospective customers and clients how good the services offered to the customer or client will be. But, their words are not always the best source of information to rely on. Checking the references of brokerages and brokers is one way to reduce the risk of getting involved with a broker who will not serve you well. It's best if you can talk to others who have had experience with the broker or brokerage that you are considering. If you are buying, make sure you talk to people who have bought from the broker. A seller might be very happy to talk to a broker where a buyer might not be. Since you are considering a co-op or condo, try to find others who have bought these types of properties from the broker you are thinking of using. Talk to a few references, not just one or two. If three to five references give good reports, you should be in suitable hands.

Brand Name Brokerages

Are brand-name brokerages better than small brokerages that don't enjoy big name recognition? If you are buying, I'd say no; if you're selling, I'd say yes. There are distinct advantages to having your home listed with a major name in your local market. The brokerage doesn't have to enjoy a national, franchise name, but it should be a productive leader in your community. Most people call on brokerages that they recognize in one way or another. If my brokerage was known as Roger's Real Estate, I certainly wouldn't expect to get the volume of customers and clients that I would as a franchised brokerage.

The fees charged by brokerages are not controlled or set. A brokerage can charge whatever amount you are willing to pay. However, most brokerages keep their charges competitive with one another. It's not likely to cost you more to list with a big-name company. Some companies that have sellers participate in the sale of their homes charge substantially less, but we will talk more about this shortly. If you are listing your home with a traditional brokerage, the commission percentage will probably be very competitive among all reputable brokerages, 5-7% of the sale's price.

Some brokerages offer special incentives, such as buy-out contracts. Basically, the brokerages guarantee to buy your home if they don't sell it. Don't expect full market value under such conditions, and don't be blinded by the fluff. If a brokerage buys your home, you can probably assume that you sold at a price well below appraised value.

Just because a brokerage has a big name doesn't necessarily mean that it will be able to sell your home faster or for more money. This is a trap into which some sellers fall. It is likely that a national name with a large sales force will produce a sale faster than a mom-and-pop brokerage, but there is no guarantee of it. You should look into the track record of any brokerage with which you are considering doing business. This will tell you what you need to know.

There are several advantages to listing with a name-brand brokerage, however. If the organization is a national operation, referrals come in from all over the country. If a seller in Denver is moving to Atlanta, the franchise owner in Denver will try to hook up the moving party with a franchise in Atlanta. As a seller, this works to your advantage. You get more activity than you might with a local broker who doesn't have long-distance contacts.

Set a Fair Sales Price

Setting a fair sales price is critical to a fast and profitable sale. Some brokers might try to list your home at a low price, just to make a quick sale. This is not in your best interest. Other agents might fluff you up with a higher sales price to get your listing. If the price is not realistic, this hurts both you and the brokerage. The agent gets credit for an all-important listing, but you don't benefit from the higher price. Ultimately, you will probably be approached by the agent and asked to lower your price. In the meantime, you've lost valuable sales opportunities. You must insist on giving a listing at a fair market value.

Have Your Home Appraised

How do you know what is a fair market price? You can pay to have an independent appraisal of your home. This is the most accurate method of establishing the value of your home. If you would prefer not to spend the money for this service, you can ask your potential broker to provide you with a current market analysis (CMA). The work done by the agent will normally involve the use of MLS data in compiling data on comparable properties that have sold in you area within recent months. You should personally review the comparable properties used to arrive at a fair figure for your home. The sales used in the comparison should be as similar to your home as possible.

Never accept a pure opinion of value that is not substantiated by documented sales. If a broker sells you on a low price, so that your home can be sold quickly, you will lose money. If the price you are given is inflated, to make you sign with one company over another, you will suffer from having your home on the market for longer than it should be. The only price to settle on is a fair and accurate one. I strongly suggest that you invest a few hundred dollars in a professional appraiser, but at the very least, insist on documented evidence of a CMA.

A Sales Plan

Before you sign a listing for your home, ask to see a written sales plan. How will the brokerage promote you home? Will you home be advertised in local media on a regular basis? Can you expect to see television ads for your property? Will the listing be placed in an MLS? Does the brokerage co-broke with other brokerages? Some brokerages are very protective of their listings and don't like to work with co-brokers. When a co-broke deal is done, the listing agency usually gives up half of the commission that you are charged. You should deal with a brokerage who will give you MLS exposure and who will co-broke with other agencies.

Average Days on the Market

When you are rating brokerages, you should find out what the average number of days on the market their listings have. In other words, do their listings sell in thirty days, forty-five days, or six months. This information can be seen in the comp books published by the local MLS. Don't accept an agent's word on the times of sales. Insist on seeing independent records that support what the broker tells you. If a broker is unwilling to share past sales records with you, it's probably a good time to seek out another brokerage.

Reserve the Right to Retract Your Listing

Listing agreements come in different configurations, but they can be very restrictive. For example, you may be asked to commit to one exclusive brokerage for a full six months. In one way, this is fair. If a brokerage works hard and spends money to promote the sale of your home, a reasonable amount of time is needed to make a sale. On the other hand, if you sign up with a lazy brokerage, you could be trapped for months. Tie your listing agreement to the marketing plan. Have a clause that allows you to withdraw your listing if the brokerage doesn't perform according to the written guidelines of the sales plan.

GETTING YOUR HOME READY TO SELL

Getting your home ready to sell can take a little time. To get the most out of your home, you need to make it as nice and as appealing as possible. People who live in a place tend to get used to it. As time passes, some of the qualities of a dwelling can deteriorate, but many owners don't notice the gradual changes. Someone who is seeing the living space for the first time will pick up on the problems quickly. You should make sure that your home will show well to perspective buyers.

It may be hard for you to be objective in your view of possible problems in your unit. A good listing broker will point out areas that need attention, but a lot of brokers won't. Many listing brokers are afraid to say anything negative to a seller. If your broker doesn't bring up the subject, you should ask the broker for an objective, professional opinion. Another way to test the condition of your home is to invite some friends or business associates over with the understanding that they will be honest in their views of your home. Still, it can be difficult to get people you know to say bad things about your home, even if it is constructive criticism.

Common sense tells you that your home should be clean and neat when you are ready to have it shown to prospective buyers. This step is simple enough, but there is more to consider. Look in your kitchen cabinets. Are the items stored there organized? Your cabinets should look as spacious and efficient as possible. Clean out some of the items if the cabinets look cluttered. Make sure all items in the cabinets are placed neatly. You can almost make a certain bet that prospective buyers who are seriously interested in your unit will open the cabinets.

Check all of your plumbing fixtures to see that they are clean and in top working order. If you have a faucet that drips, have it fixed before you put your home on the market. Any evidence of repair problems or negligence can turn a buyer off or trigger a low offer. You should go through your condo or co-op with a room-by-room inspection. Pretend that you are thinking of buying the unit, and see if the condition meets with your approval.

Should you have the walls of your unit painted before you open your door to prospective buyers? A fresh coat of paint can make a strong impact on a buyer, and painting is something that many people can do themselves. Even if you have your unit painted by professionals, the cost should be manageable, and the results could lead to a faster and better sale.

If you have lived in your unit for a long time, the floor coverings might have become rundown. Should you replace your flooring? Unless the floors are in very bad shape, I would not replace them. The new owners of your unit might want a special type or color of flooring. Having all new flooring installed can get expensive, and you may not recover the cost in your sales price. An alternative is to have the flooring cleaned professionally. There are times when installing new flooring is justified, but normally it is not necessary.

Making major improvements to your unit prior to selling is probably not a good idea. However, adding some accents can make a lot of sense. For example, look at your light switches and the electrical outlets. Are they protected with the typical, plastic covers? How would they look with brass or oak cover plates? This is a simple change that you can do yourself, and the cost doesn't amount to much. The visual effect you achieve can be just enough to catch a buyer's attention and hold it.

Small decorating moves and accents can have a big effect on a buyer. For example, adding some wallpaper to look like a stenciled boarder around the walls of your kitchen can change the appearance of your kitchen. A few new light fixtures can make your unit look more modern. New hinges and pulls on your kitchen cabinets can change the mood of your kitchen. Installing a few plug-in, under-cabinet lights in the kitchen can brighten the counter workspace and the room. Switching from plastic bathroom accessories to oak ones can set a new tone. There is a lot that you can do with a small amount of money to set your unit apart from competitive properties that are for sale.

Don't get carried away with your home improvements. Much of what you do will not increase the appraised value of your home. The modifications should make your home more attractive and desirable, but don't expect them to justify a much higher price. People sometimes over-improve to a point where they lose money, and you don't want to fall into this group.

WHEN THE SHOWINGS START

When the showings start, there are little things that you can do to help your broker make a faster sale. Talk with your broker and coordinate a plan for showings. Does the broker want you available for questions, or is it better if you are not in the unit when it's shown? Most brokers find it easier to work with customers when the seller is not present during a showing. If you have a pet, decide what will be done with the animal during showings. It's not appropriate to have a cat roaming the rooms of your unit while a showing is going on. Perhaps you can keep your pet confined in a kennel box or some other acceptable location to avoid confrontations during showings.

> **INSIDER TIP**
>
> *If you have a pet, make sure the animal is out of the way when your home is being shown to perspective purchasers.*

Many brokers arrive at a showing in advance of the prospective buyers. This gives the broker a chance to prepare the property. Ask your broker if you should leave your curtains open or closed. Should the lights be left on, or will the broker turn them on before the customers arrive? Little details often have a lot to do with the success of a showing. The more you work out with your broker in advance, the better your chances will be for a quick and profitable sale.

ONCE YOU GET AN OFFER

Once you get an offer from a buyer, you are likely to be excited. Don't let the excitement take over your senses. Read the offer carefully. Have your broker go through the offer, line by line, and explain it to you. Before you sign it, have your attorney review it. Depending on the offer, you may have a need to make a counteroffer. This is something that is usually done between a seller and a listing broker, but it's a good idea to check with your lawyer if the counter is complex in any way.

Your broker and attorney should provide you with plenty of protection if you allow them to. For example, your professional help should not allow open-ended contingency clauses. A time limit should be placed on each contingency that has to be removed. Other key items, such as the earnest-money deposit and closing date should be cleared with your broker. Talk with your professionals to see if you want to add anything to any offer you receive, but remember this, the moment you alter an offer, it becomes a counteroffer. This means that the buyer is no longer committed to the original offer. Before you change anything, make sure you are willing to take the risk of a counteroffer.

After you've entered into an acceptable contract, you will have to wait for most buyers to obtain financing. The length of time required to close most loans varies. A closing in thirty days is possible, but many deals run as long as sixty days. Don't expect to sign a contract today and get your money tomorrow.

MAYBE YOU SHOULDN'T SELL

Maybe you shouldn't sell your home at all. Have you considered keeping it as a rental property and investment? There can be numerous advantages to keeping your condo or co-op. Usually, the longer you maintain possession of a property, the more valuable it becomes. Most homes don't appreciate a great deal in just a few years. By keeping your condo or co-op as a rental property, you can hang onto it until its value is much higher. During your holding time, you can be collecting rent to defer your costs, and you should enjoy some decent tax deductions. There are also other reasons for not selling.

Let's assume that you have decided to move to another city. You've found a great condo where you want to live, but you have a co-op that you think you have to sell before you can buy the condo. The present real estate market is slow, and sales prices are low. If you sell out now, you will barely break even on your co-op investment. Oh sure, you'll get some cash for a down payment on the condo, but your net gains on the sale will be minimal. But, you do want to move, so what are you going to do?

Assuming that it does not violate board rules and bylaws, rent your co-op to a tenant. Get a loan against the equity in your co-op to use as a down payment on the new condo. If the deal works well, your tenant will basically be paying for your co-op, and you will enjoy tax advantages and continued appreciation. When the market turns good again, you sell the co-op if you want to, or you can keep it indefinitely as an investment. Have a management company manage your co-op while you're away, and you should have very little involvement with your investment. Management companies cost money, but good ones are worth their cost.

Not everyone should become a landlord. Even when a management company is involved, the requirements of landlord responsibility can take their tolls. If you have the ability to be a landlord, keeping your condo or co-op as a long term investment can be sound thinking. It is certainly a viable alternative to taking a low sales price in a buyer's market.

HAPPY TRAILS TO YOUR HOME OWNERSHIP

Well, we've reached the end of the line. Our time together is about over. Now you should feel much more prepared to buy a condo or a co-op. Undoubtedly, you still have questions and concerns. This is natural. When you talk to brokers, CPAs, and attorneys, your fears and confusion should be put to rest. Buying your own home is a major commitment, but it is one that is hard to compare with anything else you buy. Owning your own home is special, and you can own your own home if you are willing to work for it. I wish you the best of luck in your hunt for quality housing.

GLOSSARY

ACCRUED INTEREST—earned, but unpaid interest. Example: a loan is designed to have Accrued Interest, to be paid at maturity. Interest builds throughout the term of the loan and is paid in a lump sum on the date the loan becomes due in full.

ACQUISITION COST—the sale price and all associated fees incurred to obtain a property.

ADDENDUM—a document added, or attached, to a contract, becoming a part of the contract.

ADJUSTABLE RATE MORTGAGE (ARM)—a mortgage loan allowing the interest rate to change at specific intervals for a determined period of time.

AMENITIES—in appraisal terms, Amenities are benefits derived from property ownership without a monetary value.

AMORTIZATION—the act of repaying a debt gradually with periodic installments.

AMORTIZATION SCHEDULE—a table identifying periodic payment amounts for principal and interest requirements. The table may show the unpaid balance of the loan being profiled.

ANNUAL DEBT SERVICE—the amount of principal and interest required to be paid for a loan.

ANNUAL PERCENTAGE RATE—the effective rate of interest charged over the year for a loan. Note: when discount points are paid, they increase the note rate of a loan to a higher Annual Percentage Rate.

APARTMENT—a residential dwelling contained in a multi-family building, usually rented to a tenant.

APARTMENT BUILDING—a property containing multiple residential dwellings with a common entrance and hallway.

APPRAISAL—an estimated value of a property.

APPRAISER—a person qualified to estimate a property's value.

APPURTENANCE—an item outside the property, but considered a part of the realty.

ARM'S LENGTH TRANSACTION—a transaction between parties seeking their personal best interest. Not a transaction between husband and wife, parent and child, or corporate divisions.

AS IS—a term meaning the property is accepted in its present condition, with no warranty or guarantee.

ASKING PRICE—the listed sale price of a property.

ASSESSED VALUE—a value established by an assessor for property tax purposes.

ASSESSMENT—the amount of tax charged by a municipality, or local authority, for property tax.

ASSESSMENT RATIO—a formula used to determine a property's assessed value, based on the property's market value. Example: the Assessment Ratio is 50%, a property has a market value of $100,000.00, the assessed value of the property is $50,000.00.

ASSESSOR—an individual who is responsible for determining the assessed value of real property.

ASSIGNEE—a person, or entity, to whom a contract is sold or transferred.

ASSIGNMENT—a method used to transfer rights or interest in a contract to another party.

ASSIGNOR—a person, or entity, who assigns rights or a contractual interest to another party.

ASSUMABLE MORTGAGE—a mortgage loan that may be assumed from the present mortgagor by another party. Note: when a mortgage is assumed, the person assuming the mortgage accepts responsibility for the debt, but the seller of the property is responsible for the loan if the new buyer defaults on the loan. The seller can be relieved of liability if the lender will grant a novation.

ATTACHMENT—a legal act to seize property to secure or force payment of a debt.

ATTORNEY-IN-FACT—a person, or entity, authorized to act for another in the capacity of a power of attorney. The authorization may be limited to certain aspects, or it may be general in scope with all aspects included.

BACKUP CONTRACT—a binding real estate contract that becomes effective when a prior contract is void.

BALANCE SHEET—a financial sheet showing assets, equity and liabilities in two columns where the totals of each column balance.

BALLOON MORTGAGE—a mortgage loan with a balloon payment.

BALLOON PAYMENT—a lump sum loan payment due at a specific time.

BANKRUPTCY—a court action to protect debtors who have become insolvent.

BILATERAL CONTRACT—a contractual agreement requiring both parties of the contract to promise performance.

BLANKET MORTGAGE—a mortgage covering more than one real property.

BLENDED RATE LOAN—a loan mixing the interest rate of an existing loan with the current market interest rate to arrive at an attractive interest rate for the Blended Rate Loan.

BLIND POOL—a term used to describe a group of investors placing funds in a program to buy unknown properties.

BROKER—a state-licensed individual acting in the behalf of others for a fee.

BROKERAGE—a business utilizing brokers.

BUILDING CODES—rules and regulations adopted by the local jurisdiction to maintain an established minimum level of consistency in building practices.

BUILDING PERMIT—a license to build.

CASH FLOW—used to describe the amount of money received during the life of an investment.

CERTIFICATE OF DEPOSIT (CD)—a savings account instrument requiring a minimum deposit and a specified term. Certificate Of Deposits normally produce a higher yield than a standard savings account.

CERTIFICATE OF INSURANCE—evidence from an insurer proving the type and amount of coverage on the insured.

CERTIFICATE OF OCCUPANCY—a certificate issued by the codes enforcement office allowing a property to be occupied.

CERTIFICATE OF TITLE—an opinion of title provided by an attorney to address the status of a property's title, based on recorded public records.

CHAIN OF TITLE—the history of all acts affecting the title of a property.

CHATTEL—personal property. Example: a range and a refrigerator may be found in a house, but they are Chattel, or personal property, not real property.

CHATTEL MORTGAGE—a mortgage loan secured by personal property. Example: an investor buying a furnished apartment building might pledge the furniture as a Chattel Mortgage.

CLEAR TITLE—a title free of clouds, or liens, that may be considered marketable.

CLOSING—the procedure where real property is transferred from seller to buyer, and the time when the change of ownership is official.

CLOSING COSTS—fees incurred during the closing of a real estate transaction. These fees include such items as: commissions, discount points, and legal fees.

CLOSING STATEMENT—a sheet detailing a full accounting of all sources and uses of funds in a real estate transaction.

CLOUD OF TITLE—a dispute, encumbrance, or pending lawsuit that, if valid, or perfected, will affect the value of the title.

COLLATERAL—property or goods pledged to secure a loan.

COMMON AREA—the area of a property used by all tenants or owners. Example: hallways and parking areas.

CONSIDERATION—an object of value given when entering into a contract. Example: earnest money deposit, love and affection, and a promise for a promise.

CONTRACTOR—a person, or entity, contracting to provide goods or services for an agreed upon fee.

CONVEY—to transfer to another.

CONVEYANCE—the act of conveying rights or a deed to another.

COUNTEROFFER—a rebuttal offer to a previous offer to purchase real property.

COVENANTS—promises or rules written into deeds, or placed on public record, to require, or prohibit, certain items or acts. Example: a deed may have covenants preventing the use of a home for business purposes.

CREATIVE FINANCING—any financing deviating from traditional term mortgages.

DEED—a properly signed and delivered, written instrument, conveying title to real property.

DEED IN LIEU OF FORECLOSURE—the voluntary return of a property to the lender without requiring the foreclosure process.

DEED RESTRICTION—similar to a covenant, a restriction placed in a property's deed.

DEFAULT—breaching agreed upon terms.

DEFECT OF TITLE—a recorded encumbrance prohibiting the transfer of a free and clear title.

DEFERRED PAYMENT—payments to be made at a later date.

DEFICIENCY JUDGEMENT—a court action requiring a debtor to repay the difference between a defaulted debt and the value of the security pledged to the debt.

DEMOGRAPHIC STUDY—research to establish characteristics of the population of an area, such as, sex, age, size of families, and occupations.

DEPOSIT OF EARNEST MONEY—money placed with an offer to purchase real estate to assure good faith and performance of the contract.

DISCOUNT POINTS—fees paid to a lender at the time of loan origination, to offset the difference between the note rate of the loan and the true annual percentage rate.

DISCRIMINATION—showing special treatment (good or bad) to an individual based on the person's race, religion, or sex.

DOWN PAYMENT—money paid as equity and security to cover the amount of purchase not financed.

DRAW—an advance of money, from a construction loan, to reimburse the contractor for labor and materials put in place.

DUE-ON-SALE CLAUSE—a clause found in modern loans forbidding the owner from financing the sale of the property until the existing loan is paid in full. These clauses can be triggered by some lease-purchase agreements. The clause gives a lender the right to demand the existing mortgage be paid in full, upon demand. Failure to comply can result in the loss of the property to the lender.

DUPLEX—a residential property housing two residential dwellings.

DWELLING—a place of residency in a residential property.

EARNEST MONEY—money placed with an offer to purchase real estate to assure good faith and performance of the contract.

EASEMENT—a license, right, privilege, or interest that one party has in another party's property.

EQUITABLE TITLE—an interest held by the purchaser of a property placed under contract, but not yet closed upon.

EQUITY—the value between the market value of a property and the outstanding liens against it.

ESCROW—the act of placing certain money or documents in the hands of a neutral third party for safekeeping until the transaction can be completed.

ESCROW AGENT—a person, or entity, receiving escrows for deposit and disbursement.

ESTATE FOR LIFE—an interest in real property that ends with the death of a particular person.

ESTOPPEL CERTIFICATE—a document proving the amount of lien or mortgage levied against a property.

EVICTION—a legal method for a property owner to regain possession of real property.

FAIR MARKET RENT—the amount of money a rental property may command in the present economy.

FAIR MARKET VALUE—the amount of money a property may be sold for in the present economy.

FEASIBILITY STUDY—a study used to determine if a venture is viable.

FIRST MORTGAGE—a mortgage with priority over all other mortgages as a lien.

HYPOTHECATE—the act of pledging an item as security without relinquishing possession of the item.

INCOME PROPERTY—real property generating rental income.

INSURABLE TITLE—a title to property that is capable of being insured by a title insurance company.

INTEREST-ONLY LOAN—a loan with terms requiring only the payment of interest at regular intervals until the note reaches maturity.

LANDLORD—a person who leases property to another.

LEASEHOLD—the interest a tenant holds in rental property.

LESSEE—a person renting property from a landlord.

LESSOR—a landlord renting property to a tenant.

LETTER OF CREDIT—a document acknowledging a lender's promise to provide credit for a customer.

LEVERAGE—the act of using borrowed money to increase buying power.

LIEN—a notice against property to secure a debt or other financial obligations.

LIFE ESTATE—an interest in real property that terminates upon the death of the holder or other designated individual.

LIFE TENANT—an individual allowed to use a property until the death of a designated individual.

LIMITED PARTNERSHIP—a partnership where there is a general partner and limited partners. The limited partners are limited in their risk of liability.

LINE OF CREDIT—an agreement from a lender to loan a specified sum of money upon demand without further loan application.

MAI—an appraisal designation meaning, Member, Appraisal Institute.

MARKETABLE TITLE—a title to real property free from defects and enforceable by a court decision.

MORTGAGE BANKER—someone who originates, sells, and services mortgage loans.

MORTGAGE BROKER—someone who arranges financing for a fee.

MORTGAGEE—an entity holding a lien against real property.

MORTGAGOR—an entity pledging property as security for a loan.

NET INCOME—the amount of money remaining after all expenses are paid.

NET WORTH—the amount of equity remaining when all liabilities are subtracted from all assets.

NET YIELD—the return on an investment after all fees and expenses of the deal are subtracted.

NOVATION—an agreement where one individual is released from an obligation through the substitution of another party.

PASSIVE INVESTOR—an investor who provides money, but does not provide personal services in a business endeavor.

PRO-FORMA STATEMENT—a spreadsheet projecting the outcome of an investment.

SECONDARY MORTGAGE MARKET—a system where mortgages are bought and sold by investors.

WARRANTY DEED—a deed where the grantor protects the grantee against any and all claims.

ZONING—the legal regulation of the use of private land.

Index

A

C

D

G–H

I

J–L

O

P

R

S

T

U–V

W–Z

Notes

Notes